English Teaching and the Moving Image

Andrew Goodwyn's straightforward approach to teaching about the moving image demystifies this topic and shows how it can be easily incorporated into classroom practice. Building on teachers' knowledge of teaching about advertising, newspapers and visual adaptations of literary texts, this book includes chapters on:

- Adaptations: not just the film of the book
- Teaching film
- Teaching television
- Practical work
- New technologies and the moving audience

This jargon free book will be a stimulating and useful guide to teachers and student teachers looking to improve their knowledge of the moving image and its place in the English curriculum.

Andrew Goodwyn is Senior Lecturer in English and Media Education at The University of Reading. He has worked extensively to bring the fields of Media Education and English teaching together at both national and international levels.

English Teaching and the Moving Image

Andrew Goodwyn

RoutledgeFalmer
Taylor & Francis Group

LONDON AND NEW YORK

First published 2004
by Routledge
11 New Fetter Lane, London EC4P 4EE

Simultaneously published in the USA and Canada
by Routledge
29 West 35th Street, New York, NY 10001

Routledge is an imprint of the Taylor & Francis Group

© 2004 Andrew Goodwyn

Typeset in Sabon and Gill by BC Typesetting Ltd, Bristol
Printed and bound in Great Britain by
TJ International Ltd, Padstow, Cornwall

British Library Cataloguing in Publication Data
A catalogue record for this book is available from the British Library

Library of Congress Cataloging in Publication Data
A catalog record has been requested

ISBN 0–415–30660–4 (hbk)
ISBN 0–415–30661–2 (pbk)

To Anne
For all your help, love and support

Contents

Preface

English teaching has paid some attention to the moving image since the 1930s but in the year 2000, this attention became a curricular requirement for the first time. This book aims to help teachers make the most of this belated opportunity. Although English teachers have incorporated aspects of Media Education into their teaching over the past decade or so, its presence is by no means firmly established or consistent. There are a variety of reasons for this but a very significant one has been the prescriptive and somewhat reductive nature of the National Curriculum for English in the last years of the twentieth century, burdened by an even more cumbersome and uninspiring assessment framework. The rather sudden appearance of the idea that pupils should be taught about the moving image might be viewed as just one more demand on an overwhelmed profession.

This book argues that, whatever the mixed motives for this focus on the moving image, 2000 will have been a defining moment for the subject of English. Teachers of English have always been very clear about engaging with the real lives of their pupils without allowing the grim nature of much of reality to constrain them from the exploration of our emotional and aesthetic lives. The moving image is at the centre of a rapidly developing, multi-modal culture, it plays an absolutely central role in the lives of young people; it is a genuinely exciting time. Children and young people provide plenty of evidence of their intelligent engagement with this culture. It is a consumer culture but these young consumers seem more than a match for its designs on them; they have designs of their own and in a culture where technology is providing them with creative ways to engage with cultural resources they are becoming producers in their own right.

Teachers have had precious little chance to benefit from this creative energy but there are real signs that the force of these changes is proving irresistible. The book aims to be timely in helping teachers to meet the demands of the curriculum they must teach. However, it also aims to help them go far beyond the few statements about the moving image in Curriculum 2002. English has always been considered the key school subject; in embracing the moving image as central to its future, it provides a very exciting future for itself.

Chapter 1

Moving in

The moving image finally 'arrives' in the English Curriculum

Does the study of the moving image belong in a subject with as vague a name as 'English'? Certainly many English teachers use the moving image in their teaching and even more of them enjoy the moving image as part of their cultural experience every day. Given the prominence of the moving image in twentieth century culture, and the current evidence that it seems likely to be even more dominant in the twenty-first, it may seem more peculiar that its study is not at the heart of a postmodern education. But clearly it is not. All teachers of all subjects use moving image material in their classrooms and consider this absolutely normal and, perhaps, 'natural', acknowledging its prevalence everywhere in pupils' lives (and their own), and perhaps as a result of this 'ordinariness' they feel little need to pay attention to the medium itself. There is no need to labour this point any further except to emphasize that the relatively sudden appearance of this set of statements somewhat ironically deserves some explanation:

Media and moving image texts

5 Pupils should be taught
a how meaning is conveyed in texts that include print, images and sometimes sounds
b how choice of form, layout and presentation contribute to effect (for example, font, caption, illustration in printed text, sequencing, framing, soundtrack in moving image text)
c how the nature and purpose of media products influence content and meaning (for example, selection of stories for a front page or news broadcast)

d how audiences and readers choose and respond to media.

[. . .]

9 The range of texts should include
[. . .]
b print and ICT-based information and reference texts
c media and moving image texts (for example newspapers, magazines, advertisements, television, films, videos).

(DfES: 2000)

Why should these statements appear in the National Curriculum for English in the year 2000? Why not in Art? Why not in 'Cultural Studies'? Why not let all students choose Media Studies at the age of either 14 or 16? Perhaps 'Citizenship' is the rightful place for a critical analysis of a consumer culture dominated by the moving image? And if it is going to appear in English, why suddenly start at the age of 11 given that children aged 5–11 spend many hours in front of the screen and by the time they have reached five have already absorbed thousands of hours of moving images and sounds? This highlights how arbitrary in one sense the appearance of this statement must be considered, and yet in other ways it is a quite logical outcome of a long curricular and political struggle. Certainly its appearance is potentially fundamentally important and it does need contextualizing and placing within a historical narrative.

What follows is a necessarily brief account of key developments that have led to the current focus on requiring English teachers to teach the moving image. Any such account is also partly a rationale in that it attempts to clarify certain key influences over time, but the rationale also needs summarizing as a conclusion and therefore completes this chapter. This account also intends to alert teachers to some of the key developments within the media, not in a highly technical way, but in a manner that might help them to make use of such material in their teaching. The moving image does have a very real history and at the simplest level certain texts, perhaps chiefly films, now have their own 'cultural heritage' status; it has even been seriously proposed that schools adopt this approach (see Chapter 6). This is certainly not the chief motivation for producing this book but it happens to remind us that the eternal debate about the literary canon is not the only such debate and also that it just happens to have a longer history than 'the movies'.

The moving image appearing in the English frame

The 1933 battle cry against popular culture of F.R. Leavis to 'discriminate and resist' (Leavis and Thompson: 1933) remains a seminal moment and vital starting point for an understanding of the vexed relationship between English teachers and culture, high or 'low'. The importance of Leavis' specific influence has been well documented (see for example Eagleton (1983), Goodwyn (1992a)). Although over 70 years old, the battle cry still gathers much support and with the overwhelming presence of the internet in people's lives may be about to increase its support. In simple terms Leavis argued that English teachers had to teach their vulnerable youngsters to resist the seductions of popular culture; he saw film in particular as one of the worst excesses of modern, cheap culture (for a more extended discussion see Goodwyn (1992a)). This is in no way to trivialize this concern; it is as relevant today as it was then. One aspect of teaching about the media *is* to help young people understand how it 'works' and to be active rather than passive consumers and to 'resist' when they see fit. The essential problem with Leavis' view is that his chief interest lay in creating a tiny elite of novel readers who would be the torch-bearers of high culture. This certainly might be the chief aim of a particular kind of education system but not in a society with any egalitarian principles.

The other reason for making Leavis' manifesto our starting point is that he took the advent of mass popular culture very seriously. In an ironic way he invented what became Media Studies. He was always a most earnest and even passionate critic, and one thing he certainly and rightly recognized in the early 1930s was that something profound had happened. His reaction was to fear this change and to argue that educators had a vital role to play in helping young people. Again, he was right about our vital role. However, one can also understand the nature of his fear in a time of enormous global uncertainty when fascism was on the rise. The idea of a mass media was a relatively new one but its power was becoming extremely evident. Radio had already demonstrated the power of a medium to reach 'the people' but it was always essentially a domestic, and in that sense intimate, medium.

In the approximately 20 years of moving images being shown on large screens up to 1933, the notion of a mass and very public medium became a reality. Crowds of people watching together was nothing new, of course; the difference was that they appeared to be watching exactly the same thing; every theatre performance, in contrast, is 'unique'. Any kind of film could reach a huge audience very rapidly. At that time both the political right and the left felt the potential for getting a unified message across (see Inglis (1990)). Audience theory may have moved away from this fairly primitive conception but we can see now in the revival of cinema attendance through the 1990s that audiences are groups of people who actively want to watch together. It is young people in particular who in the twenty-first century enjoy this social experience. So we can acknowledge that Leavis, and many others, had recognized a paradigm shift. His particular concern was to appeal to English teachers to do something for their pupils.

For a considerable time, at least in the grammar schools, this elitist stance was the dominant, even sole concern of English teachers in relation to all mass media, their *raison d'être* being to preserve the cultural heritage of English literature. The title of Mathieson's classic 1970s study of English teachers, *The Preachers of Culture* (Mathieson: 1975), says it all. One reason, then, why the moving image motif appears in English is that as a subject it has self-consciously addressed young people's engagement with culture of all kinds. The initial stance, retrospectively characterized as 'inoculation theory' (Halloran and Jones: 1986) – i.e. dose them with a little popular culture and they will develop a resistant strain on their own – lasted perhaps 30 years as the dominant conceptual mode. It certainly continues to influence much current practice but no longer exclusively. In the mid-1990s it was also more or less enshrined in the National Curriculum for English. The extract above reveals that the pendulum has once more swung towards a much broader conception of Media Education.

However, in the 1960s a number of factors combined to effect an important conceptual shift (Hart and Hicks: 2002, 62–4). One factor was the emergence of a visible youth culture, initially concentrated on music and radio as a provider of music. Second was the extraordinary phenomenon of television: the moving image (however crude) was suddenly in the heart of the domestic space (this will be discussed in more detail in Chapter 4). Television was first a source of yet further anxiety to English teachers and other concerned parties (politicians, parents, etc.). The moral panic scenario in the history of technological change is now well documented (there is an excellent recent overview in Livingstone (2002)). However, as television settled into domestic culture it also became a source of remarkable richness for all teachers and to English teachers in particular. It is worth considering the range that television suddenly brought to the common experience of most pupils, from news and documentary to modern drama and soap opera; the emergence of popular drama modes such as police/crime series, children's television, magazine-type programming and, of course, television advertising. It remains an irony (and one of the motivations for this book) that television now receives relatively little formal attention in school, probably a good deal less than in the 1970s and 1980s.

Whatever else, television combined all aspects of culture and so problematized simple notions of inoculation. The English teacher could thus engage much more with 'discrimination': which elements of 'TV' were worth watching after all? But this became increasingly hard to agree on and, it can be argued, began to generate what later became a more cultural analysis attitude to the media in general.

These changes to the media were certainly complemented by a profound shift in education. The 1970s brought comprehensive education and the grammar–secondary divide was brought together under one roof. Grammar school teachers of English and their secondary modern colleagues suddenly were in the same staff room. In real terms it took many years for this cultural clash to become even partially resolved when the common examination format of GCSE (in 1984) finally replaced the 'O' level and CSE models. Comprehensive education, it is worth remembering, is still quite a new idea in England and already significantly challenged by notions of specialization that may essentially undermine the original movement's key principles. The key point for thinking about the moving image is that film and television were certainly available to all sections of the population; in other words the media were to some extent a universal for all young people and the emergence of a distinct youth culture posed a new challenge to all teachers.

The comprehensive movement had many motivations and aspirations and has its own remarkable history (see Benn and Chitty (1996)). English teaching at this time embraced its ideals in its own comprehensive way. There was a gradual but profound shift from a cultural heritage, 'capital L' Literature model to a sociolinguistic model of English. The history of the Bullock Report, *A Language for Life* (DES: 1975), its construction by influential thinkers such as James Britton, Douglas Barnes and Harold Rosen, and the development of the Language Across the Curriculum movement is well documented (see Marland (1977) for a contemporary account, Goodwyn (2002a) for a more retrospective judgement). In essence, because they were so focused on shifting teachers' thinking towards their use of language and the language of pupils, they barely noticed television or film. Battling, as they saw themselves, against the elitism contained in much residually grammar school teaching and thinking, they fought on the fields of literature and print text and engineered the revolution in the recognition of speaking and listening.

But clearly, although moving image texts were having an enormous impact on society, teachers were in general very conservative in their approach. There is a classic sociological study conducted in the mid-1970s, *Mass Media and the Secondary School* (Murdock and Phelps: 1973), which does investigate how teachers were reacting to the mass media in relation to their teaching and their pupils' lives. Its findings place teachers in four categories in terms of their approaches to using mass media material. In summary these are: favourable but a rare user; deeply against and deliberately excluding; very hostile and so only a user to develop discrimination and resistance; viewing as enriching and helpful in developing pupils' general understanding (Murdock and Phelps: 1973, 33–42). There has never been a substantial follow-up study, but it might well be that these categories have remained. They also discovered that 82% of teachers in selective and 44% in non-selective schools still thought that the study of the mass media had no place in the secondary curriculum. Despite gaining considerable attention and stimulating debate, the research itself was not a stimulus to change and its impact on schooling was negligible.

But the Language Across the Curriculum movement, whatever its different motivations, was the kind of paradigm shift that leads inevitably to other changes. For example it placed enormous emphasis on the value of pupils' talk; and what did children want to talk about if not television? The socio-linguistic turn can be seen in resources produced in the 1970s such as *Language in Use* (Doughty *et al.*: 1971), a great deal of which paid attention to newspaper and magazine texts to be examined as serious texts for study in their own right. This conceptual shift is a crucial one as it signals the beginnings of what became Media Education as English teachers now had an interest in all kinds of text, the literary text being just one form, not *the* form.

But the tensions within English inevitably remained. For example, the 1970s produced the rise of film studies in secondary schools. Many enthusiastic teachers began running film clubs. English departments tried showing Olivier's various versions of Shakespeare in the school hall. A few even went as far as offering an option like 'Film' for 'O' level. But this was all in the name of Art; film was worth studying as an art form (which of course it can be, see Chapter 3). Essentially for all its apparent cultural relevance this was chiefly cultural heritage in another medium. But at least it was experimental and innovative. It also signals that media-related work has often developed in more informal settings (see Chapter 6), school so often providing a point of resistance as opposed to inclusiveness. However, the moving image was receiving direct attention, at least some of the time, for its own sake.

If there was a time when television had some prominence in school it was during the period when video rapidly emerged (Levy and Gunter: 1988) as a significant factor in school and domestic life. It had many effects, but a few are well worth recalling. Video allowed the first opportunities for 'time shift' viewing; the viewer was now in charge as opposed to the medium. It meant that film could be viewed at home, leading for a time to a significant decline in cinema attendance. For teachers both changes were extraordinarily valuable. They could now show recorded programmes in school, both 'educational' material and mainstream, and they could easily bring in film to the classroom. I would argue that this did not lead to any major intellectual shift within English apart from among a minority of teachers. Video was essentially a wonderful convenience. Equally, the acquisition by some schools of a video camera was much less revolutionary than it might have been. It did lead to some interesting experiments but editing was far too cumbersome and expensive to allow for real creative work. For many pupils the sight of themselves 'on television' was probably the highlight.

But the study of television was now a practical possibility. Len Masterman's book, *Teaching about Television* (1980), is one indicator of the change in attitudes among some educators. It is worth noting that Masterman was somewhat anti-English teachers because he saw them as far too cultural heritage-like in their stance, letting all their literary baggage get in the way. This had some truth in it but was also an exaggeration. Those English teachers who were keen to teach about television turned their attention to a wide range of programmes and genres and in an era of course work could encourage their students both to write about the media and also to try their hand at scripts and story boards. Television scripts were available in school editions, and organizations like the British Film Institute began to create resources for television as well as film. Local Education Authorities began to create Media Education advisory posts, The National Association for the Teaching of English set up its Media Education working group.

But if the rise of teaching about television can be seen as the first positive mainstream educational attention to the moving image, and therefore a sign of a significant shift in educational thinking, it was also evidence of a deepening rift in that thinking. The period of the 1980s was also that of the rise of Media Education and Media Studies. The rise was not of great significance to mainstream practice in schools, apart from in a few exceptional schools. Its significance lay ahead but it was a clear indicator of the rise of the Cultural Studies movement. This complex and often contradictory movement has its own history (see for example During (1993)). Whatever else, one of its most successful off-shoots is Media Studies, now one of the most popular, but still immensely controversial, subjects in higher education.

In secondary schools the 1980s began to polarize teachers. The rise of video and especially film on video had produced yet another moral panic. Young people clearly liked to get together to watch 'unsuitable' material, usually horror/violence but also with sexual content, and to do this unsupervised by adults. This is not to play down this issue as a real one; for parents and teachers this issue will never go away and the internet has brought it back to prominence again. Therefore, Media Education could be seen as a good idea by both conservatives and progressives, that is until a clear definition might emerge of what it was trying to achieve.

Its contested and emergent definition was a feature of the late 1980s and is ongoing. A very clear indicator of its rapid emergence is that by 1989 it appears as a part of a chapter in the Cox Report (DES: 1989), the report which defined the first National Curriculum (NC) for English. This period and its controversies are well documented (see Goodwyn, 1992). But here we enter into territory that has a very direct relationship to the 2000 curriculum and the appearance of explicit statements about the moving image. One key element was the analysis in Cox of the philosophy of English teaching and how its definitions helped to provide a conceptual base for a form of Media Education in English. Cox and his committee posited

(DES: 1989, 2.21–2.25) that there were five models of English teaching, used by all English teachers and prevalent throughout their work. These are as follows.

- A 'Personal Growth' view focuses on the child: it emphasizes the relationship between language and learning in the individual child, and the role of literature in developing children's imaginative and aesthetic lives.
- A 'Cross-curricular' view focuses on the school: it emphasizes that all teachers have a responsibility to help children with the language demands of different subjects in the school curriculum: otherwise areas of the curriculum may be closed to them. In England, English is different from other school subjects, in that it is both a subject and a medium of instruction for other subjects.
- An 'Adult Needs' view focuses on communication outside the school: it emphasizes the responsibility of English teachers to prepare children for the language of adult life, including the work place, in a fast-changing world. Children need to learn to deal with the day-to-day demands of spoken language and of print; they also need to be able to write clearly, appropriately and effectively.
- A 'Cultural Heritage' view emphasizes the responsibility of schools to lead children to an appreciation of those works of literature that have been widely regarded as amongst the finest in the language.
- A 'Cultural Analysis' view emphasizes the role of English in helping children towards a critical understanding of the world and cultural environment in which they live. Children should know about the processes by which meanings are conveyed, and about the ways in which print and other media carry values.

The discussion above has touched on Cultural Heritage (CH) and Cultural Analysis (CA), but this is the first really explicit reference to CA as if a mainstream English activity. Personal Growth and Adult Needs are really pedagogical models. Language across the curriculum, according to English teachers (Goodwyn: 1992b), is not a model of 'English'; it is a pedagogical model for all teachers. Cox included a chapter (DES: 1989, Chapter 9) called 'Media Education and Information Technology', bringing together two, then, quite distinct areas which are now converging with remarkable rapidity. They were put together in one sense rightly, however, because they were then the future. In the references to media in the first NC there is, in fact, little tension between CH and CA. Cox and his committee were very responsive to the views of the profession and very inclusive in their approach to literature. As a result they included references to media texts throughout the report and the Level descriptors. They were careful to avoid terms such as 'high quality' when referring to literary or non-literary texts, preferring a statement like, 'The range should include some works that make demands on the reader in terms of content, or length or organization or language'. They made explicit use of the BFI definition of Media Education (see below), and included this very open statement:

> We have considered media education largely as part of the exploration of contemporary culture, alongside more traditional literary texts. And we emphasize elsewhere that the concepts of text and genre should be broadly interpreted in English. Television and film form substantial parts of pupils' experience out of school and teachers need to take this into account. Pupils should have the opportunity to apply their critical faculties to these major parts of contemporary culture.
>
> (DES: 1989, 9.8)

The opportunities for moving image education were thus firmly placed within the first National Curriculum for English. However, there were proposals that Media Education should be like Language Across the Curriculum, i.e. a feature of every teacher's work. The BFI produced documents (BFI: 1988, 1989) showing how it could be made an aspect of primary teaching and all secondary subjects, as indeed it is, although most teachers do not conceptualize that they are teaching Media Education when they do; so in a fundamental sense they just teach their subjects, for example, propaganda is an issue for historians. This lobbying did not lead to any great penetration into curriculum change in other subjects. The argument in Cox to be English-specific was 'Media Education, like drama, deals with fundamental aspects of language, interpretation and meaning. It is therefore consonant with the aims of English teaching' (DES: 1989, 9.9).

The BFI in its lobbying for Media Education did produce a very influential model which certainly has been widely used. The Signpost questions set out in their Primary and Secondary documents offered a genuinely Cultural Analysis approach to media texts. They identi-fied six key areas and six key questions which are presented here in a slightly simplified form:

Agencies	WHO is communicating and why?
Categories	WHAT type of text is it?
Technologies	HOW is it produced?
Languages	HOW do we know what it means?
Audiences	WHO receives it and what sense do they make of it?
Representations	HOW does it present its subject?

(Bazalgette: 1989, 8)

There is no distinct evidence that these documents had a direct influ-ence on teachers and in the various empirical studies of teachers over the 1990s they do not refer to them (for a summary see Hart and Hicks (2002)). Their significance is chiefly indicative of the ped-agogical possibilities that Media Education began to open up and of the BFI's valuable advocacy, an advocacy now much more focused on the moving image (see below).

So almost by default Media Education did become part of the first National Curriculum for English and therefore obtained statutory status for the first time. Most English teachers appeared to accept this as both reasonable and welcome. Research at the time (Good-wyn: 1992b) demonstrated that their first priority was to maintain a Personal Growth, and therefore student-centred, pedagogy. How-ever, the Cultural Heritage model was now seen as a highly prob-lematic and narrowly conservative stance, associated with elitism and exclusion. The Cultural Analysis model, on the other hand, was seen as a very useful and much more positive approach to the study of all texts; its emergence as the most important model after Personal Growth demonstrates the willingness of English teachers to incorporate media texts into their work.

Hart and Benson's (1993) small-scale research in the early 1990s found that English departments were incorporating media work into their units of work at Key Stage 4 but they also found a great deal of uncertainty among teachers about how to approach media texts and a very limited range of topics. Both film and television were rarely a focus. In 1995 the National Curriculum revisions (DES: 1995) significantly reduced the number of references to media although

(1f) stated 'pupils should be introduced to a wide range of media e.g. magazines, newspapers, radio and television, film. They should be given opportunities to analyse and evaluate such material, which should be of high quality and represent a range of forms, purposes and different structural and presentational devices.' So the catch-22 of Cultural Heritage returned, overturning Cox's far more inclusive approach; on the one hand the statement encourages attention to a wide range of media texts and yet at the same time it demands that they be of 'high quality'. However, scattered through the Reading section of the National Curriculum for English in 1995 are frequent statements that are essentially encouraging a Cultural Analysis perspective towards any text. Certainly the enthusiastic teacher could incorporate a good deal of attention to the media and the moving image throughout Key Stages 3 and 4.

One of the more far-reaching effects of the 1995 revisions became evident in the adjustments made to GCSE syllabuses as they 'came in line'. The then curriculum body (SCAA) made it clear that assessment of Reading in English at Key Stage 4 must include 'non-fiction, media and texts from other cultures' (Schools Curriculum and Assessment Authority: 1995, 37). This almost casual remark has had some powerful effects. The simplest has been to ensure that some attention to media texts is assessed at GCSE in the reading component; the various examination boards have each devised their own approach (for an extended discussion see Hart and Hicks (2002), Chapter 4). However the nature of these texts has almost inevitably been narrow in range because testing comprehension in reading leads to selecting texts that are very print-based. Typically these have included advertisements, promotional leaflets, newspaper articles and so on. One board, the NEAB, has included media work in its course work section, allowing far more scope. Anecdotal evidence suggests that this became one of the only places in English where moving image work was creatively alive.

In a sense then, the emphasis on assessing media texts through reading comprehension has reduced the amount of focus on the moving image, possibly radically. Hart and Hicks's (2002) follow-up study to the Hart and Benson (1993) study is indicative. They observed 11 lessons identified by the teachers as media lessons; all of the teachers are already atypical in being media enthusiasts prepared to be observed, and of those 11 lessons only four made use of the moving image (see Hart and Hicks (2002), Chapter 6).

The other key factor over this period is the remarkable growth of Media Studies at Key Stages 4 and 5. In simple terms this has given far more pupils a chance to study all aspects of the media and therefore far more access to the moving image for its own sake. Ironically, however, this expansion has been another reason why moving image study has, at best, remained stagnant in English. The expansion of Media Studies has been driven almost entirely by English specialists. Case study research of this development (Goodwyn and Findlay: 2001) demonstrates this precisely and also reveals how English teachers looking for a new and exciting challenge, perhaps more relevant to their students' lives, chose Media Studies, partly to escape from the increasing prescriptions of the English curriculum. As they become increasingly successful Media Studies teachers, they teach less English and a more recent study (Goodwyn: 2003) suggests that, despite their developing expertise, they may not increase their attention to media at, say, Key Stage 3.

The sudden appearance of 'the moving image'

As indicated below, the sudden and distinct emphasis on the moving image goes, in some ways, against the recent trend. Yet it is clear from this brief and selective curriculum history that attention to the media in English has a long if tortuous history, and that at times the moving image has had its place, but that place is by no means secure and at the time of writing certainly its place in practice is relatively limited. In this section the emphasis is on explaining *why* the phrase appeared, but at the same time this begins to be a rationale for its place in the subject of English; more of that specifically below.

A number of factors have played their part in its appearance in the formal curriculum in 2000. The BFI has very effectively lobbied for this change and the production of two key documents (BFI: 1999, 2000) attests to its success (see Chapter 6). In some ways it has reduced its broad support for media education in order to concentrate on the moving image, returning home, as it were, to its original brief: to lobby for film, and especially British film.

This special lobbying is part of a more general political and economic movement perhaps usefully epitomized by the creation of a Department of Culture, Media and Sport. Put simply, entertainment is very big business and the term the 'culture industry' is now no longer a contradiction in terms. Governments are now acutely aware of the 'value' of culture, materially as well as aesthetically. One reason why the moving image has slipped into the curriculum is that this is politically supported and the emphasis is at least as much economic as educational (Jones and Buckingham: 2002). Perhaps the idea of a British film industry is still a contradiction in terms but the idea (or perhaps ideal) never quite goes away. This notion has a long history and in the future may have a place in a school curriculum in which the moving image has a secure and mainstream place. For our purposes, it reminds us that the idea of a film industry remains a powerful one in political and economic circles and should, in itself, be a part of teaching about moving image 'culture'.

In discussing media institutions beginning with 'British' it is impossible at this stage not to mention the British Broadcasting Corporation itself, although there will be a slightly more extended discussion in Chapter 4. The BBC is an extraordinary institution, seen as deeply anachronistic by many and yet somehow surviving all attempts to make it a purely commercial enterprise. Its omnipresence is remarkable and its vital place in everyday cultural life is still unparalleled. Its contribution to the development of the moving image on the small screen has been, and continues to be, enormous, as other sections in this book will demonstrate, and the fact that it has endured as a public broadcaster with a powerful commitment to education means its value has also been remarkable.

The BBC exemplifies another factor in the appearance of the 'moving image'. However dominating still, its once monolithic monopoly is long gone and the arrival of cable, satellite and more recently digital broadcasting have led to a dramatic change in media provision and to consumer/audience behaviours. It might be argued that British broadcasting is simply catching up with the North American norm of proliferating local and national channels, and there is some truth in this, but it masks a much more profound change. The revolution of video watcher, putting the viewer (and teacher) in a powerful position has been subsumed by the digital consumer, able to control from home an access to huge repositories of programming, films and other media and information texts. This image is already a kind of cliché, but its significance for teachers and parents *is* fundamental.

Also fundamental is the development of the personal computer, in which the BBC also played an ironic part. Teachers with long(ish) memories will remember, perhaps with some ironic amusement, that 'the BBC' in schools was the first consistently used computer and the first producer of 'educational' software. Back in 1989 Cox and his committee (see above) put Media Education and Information Technology in the same chapter (DES: 1989), perhaps at a loss as to where else put these then strange bedfellows. But in the age of information and communication technologies the convergences surrounding the screen are highly evident (see Chapter 6). Certainly a moving image is as likely to appear on a computer screen as on a television or cinema screen. There are many issues to discuss related to this convergence, many to do with social and cultural habits of consumers, but here one difference between the PC and the television is especially important. Essentially the PC viewer is also, potentially at least, in a producing role, no longer solely a consumer but with the capability to create anything from a simple piece of editing to an 'original' text; and although it is problematic, I will let the word 'original' stand there as it is.

However, this vision of the teenager as 'digital artist' is certainly more of a vision than a reality and no amount of technological capacity is a substitute for the 'real thing', creativity itself, but it does and will help. A few schools have been able to realize some of this potential and demonstrate that digital editing offers enormous scope; more of this in Chapters 5, 6 and 7.

Students of English

The previous section focused on the evolution of media technologies and institutions and, mostly by implication, the audience. Before moving on to another evolving institution, the subject of English, it is important to reflect on young people and their relationship with the moving image as this also demonstrates why English must embrace the moving image much more comprehensively.

One of the most valuable shifts in media research over the past 20 years has been towards a more sophisticated concept of audience in general, and in particular, a recognition that young viewers have a sophistication of their own. In education the work of David Buckingham (for example, Buckingham (1993a, 1993b, 1996, 2000, 2002)) has established the concept of the young viewer as active, engaged and frequently critical, and that teachers should acknowledge but even more importantly draw on and utilize students' media knowledge. At the same time he has been equally clear that most media producers see young viewers as both present and future consumers. In other words, teachers may need a more interactive pedagogical stance, recognizing their students' knowledge, but they still have a very real job of educating to do. Current and future pupils in English classrooms come, in the majority, from media-saturated homes. The work of Livingstone (2002) has demonstrated the presence of the screen throughout the home: there is likely to be a television in almost every room, especially a young person's bedroom, and quite young children may have their 'own' television; although this is less significant in one sense, in that they often watch television in what is a family room, but completely on their own. It is the 'young person' who retreats to the haven of their room, typically surrounded by technologies for listening to and watching music, television and film, possibly with their own personal computer and/or games console. Music in particular deserves a mention here as young people increasingly 'view' it. Radio is as omnipresent as ever but even more a background source than in the past. Plenty of principally audio products on CD and increasingly DVD now come with significant amounts of visual material as the norm.

There is still some evidence that teenagers get together to watch videos at home, usually from the horror and violence genre; although even this genre now has a very distinct teen market in which the texts seem as much concerned with parody and grisly humour as any 'genuine' horror. But the moving image has regained its social power as the resurgence in cinema attendance suggests. The whole population attends, but the 14–25 market is the largest. Film on the big screen is now more popular than ever and holds its own remarkably well considering how many other media technologies offer entertainment, particularly at home. Film for young people is clearly a very important social phenomenon.

The subject of English

We have established that teaching about the media has been a feature of English for perhaps 70 years and that, therefore, the moving image has had a presence within that area. The 1989 National Curriculum made teaching about the media statutory and the version produced in 2000 made teaching about the moving image equally statutory. However, English teaching has a long history of resistance and subversion of official policies; why should the profession itself absorb yet another challenging element? The argument is strong and clear and it begins with where the subject is now but there are some additional reasons about where it needs to go.

English is always under pressure to be something different to the profession's own wishes; for example, the late 1990s were dominated by the emergence of the literacy movement. Research over the past 15 years has demonstrated repeatedly that English remains a student-centred subject and that the Personal Growth Model is the essential model for English teachers. Its centrality has been criticized and contested (see for example Morgan (1997)) but it is still the dominant mode. It is also rather less prominent in practice than teachers believe, especially in the latter stages of schooling (see Goodwyn and Findlay (2001)). It is then what Schön (1983) has called the espoused theory of the profession and there is some discrepancy with those theories in action.

Personal Growth is best understood as a combination of principle and pedagogy. Its essential principle is egalitarian, in that everyone in the classroom should be treated equally and that mutual respect between the teacher and her pupils and between pupils themselves is fundamental. This is an idealistic position. It is also, almost inevitably therefore, in danger of being unsustainable and naive. That is why other models in a sense contest for dominance; Cultural Analysis, for example, offers social critique that will immediately acknowledge that all pupils are essentially differenced and affected by class, gender and race; equally Cultural Heritage is premised on the notion that knowledge of certain texts will give pupils cultural capital.

Personal Growth stems partly from the Romantic tradition in arguing that the individual is genuinely capable of creativity. However, it also views culture as a social (not just an individual) resource, one available to all citizens, in the way Willis (1990) has in his ground-breaking work on the cultural lives of young people. From this perspective culture is both made and enjoyed by all citizens, not only those deemed artists. Such a view is also deeply idealistic. In relation to English, this perspective suggests we all participate in culture as both critics *and* producers.

English therefore can engage with the lived culture of pupils, both as individuals with differences and as 'young people' within social groupings. English was dominated by the culture of print (and still is) for all of its history but has made several attempts to escape from this preservative function. Its main attempt has been to unite a pedagogical concern for the individual with a concern for the social construction of texts. The individual in English is not constructed as *selfish* but as *social*; the negotiation of the personal takes place within considerations of the general.

Pedagogically, therefore, English must give significant attention to moving image texts and institutions as they are arguably the most formative elements for the postmodern pupil. This pedagogy is partially made possible by the movements in English (see above) towards a socio-linguistic stance on language which therefore treats all texts as powerful. It has also been enhanced by the attention given to notions of genre and discourse, placing texts in relation to each other and to the dominant and structuring modes within the history of language and therefore texts.

In this version of English as textual studies, the cult of the individual, the great text, has been markedly reduced. Equally the notion of a received reading of any text has been discredited and replaced by a combination of reader response theory and a Cultural Analysis stance which helps to explain why received readings nevertheless exist and exert great influence. And this in turn leads to a way of understanding how cultural (and other) heritages operate. This approach undermines any notion of a 'true' Cultural Heritage while acknowledging that the idea itself is immensely powerful and for many irresistibly seductive.

In a textual studies mode, in an educational paradigm, we move from what might be called casual attention to a focused and reflective attention; we seek to explain as well as enjoy and understand. That is why the study of the moving image will be different from its mere presence in the classroom as adornment or entertainment. As suggested above, much of the media work undertaken in English has been relatively 'safe', i.e. it has tended to keep within the territory of written language, and even when using, say, television adverts, as much attention has been paid to the word, spoken or written, as to the semiotics of the visual text.

So this is where the subject itself will need to change. Its textual studies base will remain strong but the visual text should increasingly receive attention both in its own right and as conceptualized within genres. This will require a shift in expertise both as subject knowledge and as pedagogical subject knowledge (Shulman: 1986). The former is increasingly present in the subject knowledge base of English teachers joining the profession. For example, many PGCE students come from degrees which have included both linguistic and media elements; in that sense they are ready to embrace teaching the moving image. However, they do not encounter many English classrooms where the pedagogical knowledge is very evident, i.e. how to help 11-year-olds study the moving image and, even more challenging, begin to work with and create or manipulate moving images. There are supporting agencies in, for example, the BFI and Film Education but they still only reach the 'converted'.

In some ways the turn towards the moving image is already underway because, as discussed above, the computer is a powerful change agent. Here the knowledge base of the profession has most certainly altered radically. Even ten years ago (Goodwyn *et al*.: 1997) the majority of English teachers were suspicious of the computer, positioning it as a threat to traditional English work and to book reading in particular. Equally this view was arguably an ignorant one as these teachers had almost no experience with machines themselves. A combination of factors (see Goodwyn (2000)) has fundamentally changed this and both new and serving teachers have become skilled personal users, and have embraced ICT conceptually. There are still many problems with resources, access and technical frustrations (see Ofsted (2001)) but there is no resistance to ICT *per se*.

Literacy or literacies?

There are perhaps more fundamental difficulties contained in prescribed policies about Literacy that retain a 'new basics' paradigm (Lankshear: 1997). There is a notion that pupils need the basics of written language instilled before they are capable of sophisticated understandings of other media. For many pupils this leads to a downward spiral of endless 'catch up' literacy teaching that is both demeaning and disaffecting.

But this particular version of the Literacy movement of the past 15 or so years is not the only one. The research community has been arguing for both a revised notion of literacy and also for an acknowledgment that 'literacies' may be a better formulation. In the former case, the argument has been that the notion of the literate citizen is very different from even ten years ago, i.e. even at the functional level an adult cannot play a role in society without a broad capability as a receiver and creator of texts of all kinds from dense print to exclusively visual with all the multi-modalities in between. This argument has tended to produce a conservative reaction where the stance taken is that all this 'new-fangled' stuff is both a distraction and a *cause* of the problem. Familiar complaints abound about the increasingly illiterate population, a myth so powerful and persistent that it continues to survive despite all the overwhelming evidence to the contrary.

However, at the same time, there have been arguments for literacies, e.g. computer, media, latterly even emotional. These tend to come from advocacy groups determined to maximize attention for their particular concern and often this has led to intellectual in-fighting and not much else. In some countries, most notably Australia, the notion of literacies has entered mainstream educational, possibly even political thinking, and the curriculum reflects this paradigm shift. But England has a very prescriptive approach to curriculum in which the dominant mode is a simplistic concept of literacy.

Another dimension has been the emphasis of a whole-school approach towards all teachers playing a role in supporting pupils' general literacy development, and equally, that subject teachers need to address the peculiar literacy demands of their subject. This seems an entirely positive and potentially very powerful movement. Ironically, it may also allow teachers of English a fresh opportunity to review the subject. On the one hand there is renewed pressure for teachers of English to act as the guardians of literacy and to be role model literacy teachers, but, on the other, the sharing of some of this responsibility across the curriculum affords the chance to define what exactly English provides within the curriculum that other subjects do not.

From the literacies perspective, all subject teachers can contribute to the literacies of their pupils. So, as well as the written word there will be computer literacy and media literacy teaching to be done in every subject as and when appropriate, but also with some overall curriculum co-ordination and definition. But in terms of what English offers, the study of a narrative film or of television fiction make obvious and easy starting points.

And that is all they are: starting points. English will need to be the curriculum focus for teaching about how the moving image works just as it strives to teach how language works and how specialized forms of language, like novels and poems, 'work'. A good example of this need is to consider a term very familiar in English: 'non-fiction'. It reminds us that we can organize texts into fiction and non-fiction and that however loose these categories are, they can be quite helpful. Other subject areas do not deal with this distinction in any real way. Even in History, where so much attention is given to analysing sources and evidence, the real purpose is to select between non-fictions. The key point is that English is concerned with all forms of textuality, including the spoken and now the visual text, and with our response to, and understanding of, text and the creation of texts of our own.

English then is the subject in which to study and enjoy the moving image. And subjects in secondary schools, for all their curriculum documentation and definition, never have the neat boundaries that such official accounts suggest. So other subject teachers are very likely, on occasion, to make use of the moving image in a media education mode, but for the foreseeable future this can only be helpful and by no means part of *an education* about the moving image. In terms of subjects, Information Technology and Media Studies might be much greater contributors to pupils' understanding, but their mainstream influence is slight at present.

Plenty of schools now provide discrete Information Technology lessons in which pupils are taught about the internet, for example. These lessons seem to work within an operational, principally technical paradigm and tend to show pupils how to do something and, to some extent, how to make electronic texts. There is no question that such teaching is extremely useful, particularly where other subject teachers can then make use of these operational skills in their own lessons. If anything, this strengthens the argument for English to concentrate on the critical and creative dimensions of ICT in English.

As discussed above, Media Studies has grown remarkably throughout the education system, especially post-16 and, in schools, principally because of the advocacy of English teachers. But the growth of English Language Studies has had an exactly similar genesis. It seems that English is offering the foundation for a number of specialisms. In a sense they have always been there, in the territory, but as more and more students stay in education so more specialisms become possible, perhaps necessary. GCSE Media Studies is taken by a significant number of secondary pupils but it is very much an option.

English, not always for the right reasons, remains at the centre of the curriculum, still afforded a status as *the* key subject, making English teachers key figures. This is one reason why, for a significant period, and certainly for the entire lifespan of the National Curriculum, remarkable attempts have been made to define and prescribe the English curriculum in order to reduce the direct influence of English teachers themselves. Prescription undoubtedly has had a very significant effect, and research shows (Goodwyn: 2002a) that English teachers have increasingly felt boxed in and that Literacy policies are seen (whatever their intrinsic merits) as a further erosion of professional autonomy. And this is certainly one reason why student and beginning teachers do not find many established teachers developing innovative practice using the moving image; perhaps it is impressive that they find as much as they do?

Moving image, moving on

So, ironically, the English curriculum *has* to teach about the moving image while other pressures are pushing it away from developing good practice in that area. But ironies aside, there is nothing new here. This first chapter has attempted to put some of these contradictory pressures into some kind of meaningful historical perspective. It has also attempted to provide a rationale for putting the moving image into the centre of English teaching through an analysis of the philosophy of English, the culture of young people and the converging fields of technology.

Certainly English needs to move on and to renew itself in the twenty-first century. Many English teachers are profoundly frustrated by an imposed curriculum and by a model of pedagogy that they find alienating. Teaching about the moving image is not in itself a panacea but it is transformative, bringing English much more intelligently in touch with lived culture and critical energy: the remainder of the book aims to substantiate that claim. In doing so the argument will be extended and developed in each chapter and revisited in Chapter 7. The book as a whole aims to provide both a consistent argument and frequent demonstrations of current practice and, where relevant, how practice will need to change in the near future. Chapter 2 starts where many English teachers start, with the place of adaptations in the classroom: the 'book of the film' syndrome. The third chapter moves logically on from the adaptation to the more generic use of film and the fourth examines television, currently the most neglected aspect of the moving image in schools. Chapter 5 reviews the place and value of practical moving image work in English and strongly endorses both its importance and its feasibility. Chapter 6 pushes the boundaries of current work by including the internet and computer games within the brief of moving image education. The concluding chapter extends the argument about moving image education, arguing for some necessary changes to the subject of English but also recognizing that many aspects of such work offer a 'return' to the creative and imaginative paradigms of progressive English teaching. It also focuses specifically on the issue of the identity formation of young people in the digital age, and brings in their voices and those of current teachers to demonstrate just how exciting and valuable moving image work can be. It looks ahead to the near future where teaching and learning in English can once more feel much more connected to the energy and creativity of young people, principally through moving image-related work.

One final introductory point is that moving image work is part of the broader conception of media education. It would be merely pedantic to insist that all references in this book are exclusively to the moving image. English teachers work with a number of symbolic systems in an increasingly multi-modal environment of which the moving image is increasingly the most important. The book therefore concentrates on the moving image but constantly acknowledges the value of media education in English as the conceptual context in which such work takes place.

Chapter 2

Adaptations
Not just the film of the book

This chapter explores the concept, chiefly, of visual adaptation and argues that English teachers should teach the concept itself and move away from an essentially literary approach in which the adaptation is merely a useful but problematic teaching aid for the 'superior' original. To support this argument, the chapter reinforces some of the arguments of Chapter 1 about how our definition of literacy is changing and relates this to ongoing changes in the history of English teaching. The chapter then reviews issues to do with the nature of adaptation, puts forward a new conceptual position for teachers and then offers a range of examples that show how this might work in practice. The emphasis here is not on teaching film *per se*: that is the focus of Chapter 3. The logic of this relates to English teachers and their concern with teaching literary texts and the relationship of such texts to 'versions' of those texts. Perhaps an interest in teaching about film itself is more likely to develop from work on adaptations than from any other approach? It is also still the case that very few teachers of English would take the bold step of treating a film as a text for study in its own right, partly because the curriculum itself and its prescriptions militate against such an approach. The other reason for, in a sense, 'avoiding' film appears to be teachers' lack of training and confidence. These factors are at least likely to disappear over time. In every sense then, starting with adaptations makes very good sense.

The main focus in this chapter, given that this is a book about the moving image, is on how English teachers can incorporate visual adaptations into their classrooms, although audio adaptations clearly also have a role. Typically, an adaptation is a text that has been created to suit a particular medium, for example film, and which is based on another text, originally conceived for a different medium, most frequently a novel. This focus in itself is not new; making use of adaptations to teach literary texts is a well-established pedagogic tradition. However, what might be defined as current methodology needs a radical change and the focus of our teaching should be *the concept of adaptation*. The reason for this change stems from our requirement to address the everyday needs of future citizens of the twenty-first century. Although much contested, our concept of literacy is itself undergoing a radical change and the scope of this new concept, increasingly characterized as multi-literacies (see Chapters 1 and 6), leads us inevitably towards a new approach to teaching about texts. For reasons outlined below, using adaptations in the classroom can help us to work towards this essential transition to multi-literacies.

Adaptations – the old donkey and carrot model

Our current classrooms are sites where the literacy battle can be seen and felt. English teachers are experiencing the pressure from the conservative and traditional forces desperate to maintain the nineteenth-century model of literacy while being pulled towards the new model by their pupils' needs and by the experience of their daily lives (see Goodwyn (2002a)). It is inevitable that these two forces contend most fiercely over literary texts, especially those with traditional canonical status. How can English teachers cope with this struggle? Unfortunately no-one has a neat, satisfying answer. However, we can focus on an area that is clearly increasingly central to English teachers' work and that will help both pupils and teachers feel more positive and prepared for the world of multi-literacies.

It may be helpful first to analyse the struggle as epitomized in many classrooms by the existing 'donkey and carrot' approach to teaching a literary text. The teacher has a text to teach, for whatever reason, and also has access to a video version of a recent (or often not so recent) adaptation. She may initially interest the class by showing them a snippet of the video, usually selecting an especially effective visual moment and then explaining that the class will study the written text, the original, and that they will be allowed to view the video if the class is working well. The donkey has seen the carrot and so begins the plod through the text, and as progress is made he receives a few more mouthfuls of carrot with the prospect of the possible feast at the end of watching the whole video.

We all know that this approach 'works'. We can get our pupils to read at least some of the original and, by concentrating on studying the writing, they will not become too confused by the 'poetic licence' taken by the director, who has usually 'messed up' the original. In the age of video, cable, satellite and digital broadcasting, the internet and the CD-ROM, this approach may be seen as both somewhat primitive and also misleading for pupils and the teacher. Such an approach might simply be used in a more sophisticated way and there is no intention here to ignore the practical challenges of class-room discipline. The moving image is a very powerful attention 'grabber' and, if we are honest, pacifier and in that way will have its very real 'uses'. However, even a more sophisticated version will tend to reinforce the limits of this practice and very little educa-tion about the moving image is likely to be possible. There are several key issues.

First, it perpetuates the myth that the written text is not only the original but is also the only valuable version of that narrative, therefore the 'visualization' is a simple and easy version. Second, this approach transmits to pupils the idea that reading literature is always hard and dull while watching is easy and enjoyable. Of course, skilful teachers overcome many of these simple assump-tions, but fundamentally we may remain trapped in a textual prison, partly of our own making. However, it is much fairer for us to see such a teaching approach as essentially an intelligent reaction to the current transition; then we can also see that it owes most to a nineteenth-century model of reading; it is only a short-lived compromise. Currently, literature teachers have little opportu-nity to learn how to teach media texts (see Goodwyn (1992a), Hart and Benson (1992), Hart and Hicks (2002)), but this will certainly change.

The Age of Narrative?

It is important to step back from individual texts and their adapta-tions and to consider how English teachers are generally positioned as the literacy transition gathers speed. Research about their views suggests that teachers can still express deep anxieties about the coming computer and information age (see Goodwyn *et al.*: 1997) chiefly in relation to its perceived negative effect on reading. The first issue is conceptual. The perception among many literature teachers is that, in the so-called 'information age', technological change will undermine the importance of print and therefore the book and ultimately literature itself. The result is the feeling that literature is under attack and so must be defended. It does seem likely that print, in its literal physical sense, will become less dominant (see Tuman (1992), Lanham (1993), and Chapters 6 and 7). However, if we conceptualize literature as made up of words in various combinations then it is possible to recognize that we are essentially a *verbal* as opposed to *print* species. Electronic communication has vastly increased output of both the written and the spoken forms. Technology has hugely increased our output of all kinds of visual images. Humans demonstrate an insatiable appetite for words, images and narratives and almost every new technological breakthrough enhances our capacity to produce and receive them in multifarious combinations. So, perhaps ironically, the information age is actually producing the narrative age: information for most people, it can be argued, is for work and merely survival; narrative is for living and well-being. The English teacher, the knower and orchestrator of narratives, is actually in a quintessentially powerful role.

Many literature teachers respond by arguing that proliferation is not improvement, that more does not mean better and may, indeed, mean worse: a traditional and powerful elitist argument, influentially expressed to the English-speaking world by Leavis (see Leavis and Thompson (1933), and Chapter 1) and his many followers, although there is currently no actual evidence that the world is becoming a less literate or less sophisticated place. However, our definitions of culture are changing and as more people have opportunities to engage with popular culture in all its forms, this engagement, rather than the mere technology that provides it, marks a transition and potentially an end to literature as it is currently understood.

In schools, at present, English teachers are faced with a dilemma: teaching either nineteenth- or twenty-first-century literacy. In the new model, literature will continue to play a crucial part but not *the* crucial part. For many of our future pupils, the greatest textual experiences will come from a whole range of media. Books will play their significant part. Pupils' initial contact with many long-lived and well-loved stories will come through an adapted form. Though this is not a problem, it challenges us to continue to make our transition. The key argument is that literature teachers will become textual teachers (see Scholes (1985), Goodwyn (1992a)) and, to ease the transition, adapt and evolve.

Adapting to the novel

The donkey and carrot approach to using adaptations is an understandable compromise but is now out of step with our collective needs. That is not to say that using an adaptation chiefly to support the teaching of a literary text is simply misguided: at times this would be entirely appropriate and teachers must be trusted to make their own professional decisions about methodology. However, as this approach currently dominates English teaching, a challenge must be proposed.

The first step is conceptual. English teachers could think less about individual texts and more about *adaptation as a concept in its own right*. In other words, we should be teaching about adaptation as a process and helping pupils to understand it through both analytical study and practical work. Such an approach should develop, especially in older pupils, some understanding of the wider cultural and economic implications of adaptations in a global, electronic market (see Buckingham (1993a, 1993b)). Ultimately, the aim of such work is to go beyond an understanding of the process of adaptation to a critical position in which future citizens can reflect on *the significance* of adaptation.

There is an argument therefore that pupils do not simply learn about adaptations or 'how it is done'; they need to investigate and explore the concept. The term itself, coming from the Latin for 'suitable' has a positive connotation. Referring to someone as adaptable is complimentary; we mean that she is able to change in a positive way. Behind some of this thinking is the biological concept of evolution; change is a necessary part of remaining a healthy species. However, there is nothing necessarily positive about change: catastrophes also induce change. Equally, adaptations of a text may be considered catastrophes! In one sense, they seem less like biological change because human agency is involved; the process requires at least one adapter. For pupils, understanding the scope of human agency is very important. For example, an 'adapter' is subject to many external forces (social, cultural, political, economic, intellectual) that may or may not lead to the realization of the adaptation itself.

So, although the term 'adapt' may have a positive connotation, neither the process of adapting a text nor the reactions of an audience will necessarily result in positive experiences! In fact, a key element in working with pupils on adaptations is the capacity of such 'hybrid' texts to produce dissatisfactions and unease. One useful way of helping us, as teachers, to think about this is conceptualized by John Thompson. He notes that 'the adaptation phenomenon has always made people uneasy' (Thompson: 1996, 11), and argues that

> there is a tangle of grounds for unease – I am thinking of considerations of 'authenticity' (the original is authentic, the adaptation is a simulacrum), of 'fidelity' (the adaptation is a deformation or dilution of the original), of art-form 'specificity' (the literary original, if it is valuable must unfold its material in terms of distinctive literariness, and this must be lost in a filmed version, while the film version itself represents a lost opportunity to develop material of a specifically filmic sort) and of 'massification' (the original must be harder, more cognitively demanding, than the adaptation, or the latter would not be the more popular form for a mass audience; but then the easy access to the material must involve deskilling the reader/viewer).

This summarizes the unease felt by many teachers of literature and helps us see the sources of our own negative reactions and irritations. However, it also helps us to see that our reaction is predicated on knowledge of the 'original' written text. We may need to recognize this as a form not of knowledge but of prejudice.

The other issue for teachers is their personal motivation for engaging with an adaptation. In the same chapter, J. Thompson (1996, 12–16) discusses at length the work of Harriet Hawkins, who analyses *Gone with the Wind* at some length. In discussing that adaptation, she herself quotes from a review of the film version of Tom Wolfe's *The Bonfire of the Vanities* in which reviewer Richard Corliss comments:

> Novel readers are a possessive lot because they have already made their imaginary film version of the book – cast it, dressed the sets, directed the camera. In many cases, so have the novelists themselves: De Palma's film flopped because Tom Wolfe had already created a great movie in the minds of his readers.

This seems to be a simple but very perceptive point with several elements to it. The first must relate to the nature of the 'realization' of the narrative by the reader. The term most English teachers would refer to would be 'imagination'. That is, whatever the author's written blueprint, the individual reader must 'realize' the book. This could take us in many directions from reader response theory to psychoanalysis, but for our purposes it is best to stay within the English teachers' territory. In that territory, 'imagination' is a very powerful and evocative term. It is, for example, a term used as the highest form of praise for very able pupils in the subject (see Goodwyn: 1995). 'Imaginative' is a term to be found consistently through official documentation about the subject in most English-speaking countries as a desirable characteristic of pupils themselves but principally of *their writing*. English teachers then are very concerned with the imagination particularly in relation to fiction and encourage their students both to read it and to write it.

It is important to trace this back to their own formative reading. The evidence, based on accounts by student teachers of English, is that the notion of a 'love of reading' is fundamental to their later professional identities (for a full analysis see Goodwyn (2002b)) and it has many emotional associations in early childhood to do with comfort and pleasure and in adolescence to do with intellectual excitement and self-discovery. Imaginative fiction has thus been hugely important to English teachers, and this includes a subconscious level. Not surprisingly, they are very good indeed at 'realizing' books in this way; their imaginative powers have become highly developed. To return to Corliss' comment, they are a 'possessive lot', the novels they have read and realized are rather like their own fully formed film versions; it might even be argued that they have already, therefore, 'seen the film'.

It must be noted that all readers do this to some extent and also that some novels may be much more 'realizable' as a film than others. For example, in her discussion of *Gone with the Wind*, Hawkins comments about the director, Selznick's, view of the original novel:

> From his first reading . . . Selznick realized that, in visual details, dialogue and costuming and characterization, Margaret Mitchell had imagined a great movie. He therefore wanted the film to seem like an exact photographic reproduction of the book, including 'every well-remembered scene' either in 'faith-

ful transcription of the original' or in keeping with the spirit of Miss Mitchell's book.

(J. Thompson: 1996, 13)

Clearly some novels are very visual in their level of detail; others very deliberately less specific. It must also be recognized that the novel writers of the past hundred years have been progressively more exposed to and possibly influenced by films; inevitably some writers may now have the film version in mind and construct their novels accordingly. All of these points might be used in appropriately contextualized ways by teachers and pupils as part of their exploration of the concept of adaptation.

However, to return to our main point, English teachers are likely to choose adaptations of an original that they have already fully 'realized' and, being highly developed 'realizers', are likely to encounter the various forms of 'unease' that Thompson articulates above. The key point for them is to acknowledge this for what it is: that is an essentially learned response. It is also a response derived from being a highly skilled reader of imaginative fiction and much less as an 'appreciator' of film. Some of their pupils may be in the opposite position at least in terms of implicit knowledge, i.e. more skilled at reading films than novels.

Mutatis mutandis ('With necessary changes')

Another, perhaps playful, conceptual point can be considered here before discussing some examples and some practical approaches to classroom work. To extend the earlier metaphorical speculation about biological change, it can be suggested that texts, rather like species, can be viewed as changing and *being changed*. It is helpful to look at texts as dynamic entities, under pressure to change in a number of ways and to explore this concept through the metaphors from biology of adapting and mutating.

Mutant, though variously defined in various dictionaries, generally assumes that an organism has undergone sudden and remarkable change. In earlier definitions in modern European languages it had to do with musical change (for example, a mutation stop on an organ or changes to syllables in Germanic languages). Currently 'mutant' conjures up images from a range of typically visual texts, from the science fiction and horror genres, in which monstrous creatures have been produced through pollution or radiation; this equates mutants with unnatural and catastrophic changes and with our collective guilt about the way we may be abusing our planet. To adapt, however, is, as partially argued above, to change in harmony with the environment, to fit in, in a positive sense.

An adaptation (in the textual sense) suggests that a human agent or agents transfer a text from one medium to another. This gives the impression that individual human artists remain at the centre of this adaptive process. Mutation, however, suggests that powerful, usually inhuman, forces have caused change. What might it mean in the textual environment?

Perhaps a combination of mutation and adaptation provides a more accurate description. In the English speaking world in the 1990s, Jane Austen's work was very prominently adapted. In one such case, Emma Thompson adapted and also starred in *Sense and Sensibility*. What makes her text unusual is that many readers of the film actually might know she adapted it but only because she is also a 'star' in the traditional, Hollywood, sense of the term. Most audiences watching *Sense and Sensibility* would consider it to be by Jane Austen and would be unaware of the 'adapter'.

First then, literature teachers could usefully extend their repertoire by engaging pupils with the concept of adapters and adaptation, not just using the film of the book but actually exploring adaptation as *a phenomenon in itself*. This, expressed simply, is a shift from the 'film of the book' to the interrelationship of two texts and an examination of that relationship. It also requires a recognition that there are other, almost invisible texts, such as the original treatment for a film (a kind of overview or summary of the filmic version), the screenplay, the story boards and so on; many of these texts may never be available in the public domain. However, the internet, through film and fan sites, is making them more accessible, and DVD technology in particular means that films often come with a wide range of additional texts that are excellent material for teachers and pupils.

These 'other' texts have their own conventions and challenges for teachers and pupils (see Chapter 3). For example, screenplays are very much working scripts and are never intended for publication. They have none of the literary status of the 'manuscript' or first draft. Hollywood in particular is legendary for its disregard of writers and for the merciless way it discards scripts (and script writers) and simply 'buys' another one. As a result, film credits often reveal a list of writers' names and also a kind of hierarchy of responsibility/authorship. A few screen writers have published their scripts, especially if they are also better known as writers of novels or plays. Very often the published script varies considerably from the actual film, even to the dialogue spoken; films are not made or edited in the relatively insular way that novels are written, revised and published. Scripts have to be 'realized'; they can be very simple in appearance yet complex to read because, whereas novels are (usually) readerly, scripts are perhaps 'actorly' or even 'directorly'. Many things happen to films once they go into production, leading to major changes during production as well as at the editing stage. Not the least of these factors will be the budget: films are famous, or perhaps infamous, both for being ruined by accountants and sometimes for ruining the accountants themselves. A sudden change in world events may dramatically alter the way a script is realized as the producers, and possibly everyone else involved in the film, attempts to adapt it to help it 'survive'.

To some extent this is just teaching pupils about the complexities of film-making and the whole messy process by which a very glossy film is made. However, teaching the concept of adaptation means that a particular novel will be investigated as to how it has been adapted and the nature of the adaptive process. This means exploring more than just the human and aesthetic dimensions and bringing in the larger, relatively impersonal, forces that affect the creation of texts.

In this sense, adaptations may also perhaps be treated as mutant texts. In a sense the 'original' literary text is itself the first adaptation. The vision of the world offered by any artist is a representation of reality, not reality itself, and is necessarily moulded by the social and cultural context of its production. Writers may adapt to this context in a confirmatory or innovatory way, but they are essentially situated within an evolutionary stage in terms of language and consciousness, and work within the parameters of these constraints. For example, Dickens's novels may be seen as a powerful critique of Victorian life but they are essentially part of that life. Subsequent readaptations produced in a different historical and social context, for a new audience, work with different conceptions of social experience. Thus the text will undergo changes due to a translation from a purely verbal to a visual/filmic/televisual/dramatic medium; it will also be altered by the external, even impersonal forces which exert their power on the text. The adaptation can thus be viewed as a kind of nexus where positive and negative forces collide and compete, allowing us to ask, 'How has this new form been produced?' For example, the film *To Kill a Mocking Bird* is seen by many as both a good film and a 'faithful' adaptation. Nevertheless some key differences emerge, one being that Tom Robinson, the black character victimized by white society, is viciously gunned down in a hail of bullets in the novel but in the film he is 'tragically' killed by one bullet that was intended only to wound him. Pupils can analyse this change for what it reveals about the implied audiences of the original book and film.

Patsy Stoneman's book *Bronte Transformations: The Cultural Dissemination of Jane Eyre and Wuthering Heights* (1996) provides an extraordinary account of the literally hundreds of adaptations that have been made. She argues that not only do 'people transform texts . . . and texts transform people,' but 'texts transform themselves' (Stoneman: 1996, 1). She analyses how these texts have gone through infinite reinventions. *Wuthering Heights* particularly has been subjected to diverse emphases to reflect the nature of Heathcliff and Cathy's love as either conventionally romantic or sexually subversive. Pupils are in this way invited into the creative process of adaptation by reflecting on why certain texts have a history of adaptation. In some cases, as with *Wuthering Heights*, the text has been adapted across many media, leading to a potential category of meta or plastic texts that somehow offer infinite adaptability.

Equally, adaptations reveal a great deal about the social context of a period. For example, when Thackeray's *Vanity Fair* was serialised in England by the BBC as one of its 'classic serials' (broadcast in the autumn of 1987) it was chosen partly because it seemed to offer some critique of modern, Thatcherite Britain (Giddings *et al.*: 1990) and, at the same time, had to be an authentic period drama reflecting the manners of the original era. It also had to be exportable for family audiences around the world. Though Thackeray himself had conformed to Victorian readerly expectations, the directors of the serial had to acknowledge changes in viewer expectations and conform themselves to the definition of 'family viewing' in the late 1980s. The case study of *Vanity Fair* in *Screening the Novel* (Giddings *et al.*: 1990) provides a rich picture of the myriad forces interacting with this adaptation. Simply placing it within the 'classic serial' slot meant that particular commercial forces were at play. Classic serials have been defined as

The production of a mythologised British 'history'; and 'tradition' . . . in strictly domestic economic terms [they] are expensive but become 'a good investment' when guaranteed foreign sales are involved. The marketing of British culture as a televisual commodity has become almost a corollary of the British tourist industry, and fulfils a similar role in international terms.

(Gardner and Wyver, quoted in Kerr (1982))

Pupils could gain an understanding of such television adaptations by considering the technical and media interests; for example, television adaptations have a very different timescale to films, i.e. many episodes, usually of exactly the same length, and they may be designed to 'fit' particular slots whose conventions they must address. Other issues concern the interplay between commerce, cultures and audiences.

Emma Thompson's *Sense and Sensibility* is both a readaptation and also a mutant text. Not just different from the original novel, it also varies from other visualizations and dramatizations produced this century. Thompson's *Sense and Sensibility: The Diaries* (E. Thompson: 1996) reveals the actress/director dealing with a wide range of processes to create a 'good film' that qualifies as both a good adaptation and a commercial success since the production was financed with US money. Austen's *Pride and Prejudice*, considered her most popular novel, has existed in even more mutations. The main point is that external, even impersonal, forces have exerted their power on these texts. Literature teachers, unless still under the spell of the ahistorical New Critics, would almost certainly want to look at the social and historical context in which Austen's *Pride and Prejudice* or Dickens's *Great Expectations* were produced. Adaptations provide another challenging layer of complexity. The new text is formed through a kind of renegotiation between the author and the adapter, both struggling with the other's unfamiliar cultural context.

Classroom practices

This understanding of the complexity and richness of adaptation can be translated into classroom practice in a number of ways. Teachers commonly ask their classes to consider a novel's 'adaptability'. Questions about genre, setting and suitable players for the various characters make useful starting points. However, as with the use of the novel *Heart of Darkness* in the film *Apocalypse Now*, pupils might consider how a basic narrative could reach an audience in a particular way. Equally, considering the Hollywood-style *Clueless*, wittily based on *Emma*, provides a source for judging where an adaptation should have a 'close fit' or where significant changes might be made. These general questions lead pupils into writing scripts, visualizing scenes and trying out various interpretations.

In small groups, pupils can consider competing adaptations of a text, 'selling' their version to other pupils, role-playing financiers and/or producers. This introduces the idea of mutation: what forces make a particular text become relevant to a new time frame? In the same way, pupils can consider the endless recycling of texts such as *Dracula* and *Frankenstein*. These texts are reimagined by, it seems, each generation and each version is inflected by that generation's angst. Pupils might speculate about what the next version will be like, what forces will influence the text and what issues may be appropriately explored within its particular tradition. Younger pupils can examine how television for children adapts and recycles key heroes such as Superman, Batman and Spiderman. Hollywood blockbuster versions of these cartoon figures provide an intriguing form of adaptation and an opportunity for pupils to see historical processes at work. Questions such as 'Where does Superman come from?'; 'Why did the twentieth century invent him?'; 'Why do all the females, like Superwoman, appear later than the males?', help pupils to gain a perspective on a wider cultural world.

This approach leads, very appropriately, to an examination of the idea of the original literary text and a consideration of why it was produced at a specific historical moment. Contrasts between Lawrence Olivier's 1940s film, *Henry V*, made as part of the war effort in the Second World War, and Kenneth Branagh's 1990s, post-Falklands version provide excellent examples. Branagh clearly makes an auteur statement in response to Olivier; one world famous actor–manager consciously follows another, not only taking the same, 'original' text with its very powerful national resonances at a time of nationalistic anxiety, but also making a claim for his predecessor's pre-eminent status (as Shakespeare's Henry V does to his own father, Henry IV). After considering why Branagh and Olivier produced *Henry V*, pupils can apply the same question to Shakespeare's work. This may be a far more meaningful way to help pupils 'appreciate' Shakespeare, especially if they also learn that *he adapted all his material from other sources*.

When Kenneth Branagh directed *Frankenstein* he claimed to have gone back to the original text and so entitled the film *Mary Shelley's Frankenstein*. This simple act of 'reclaiming' provides an excellent focus for a class looking at concepts of adaptation and originality. It also provides an excellent means for pupils to reflect on the fascination with certain 'modern' myths, e.g. the created but destructive monster, the inhuman/human and their varying representations through print, stage and screen.

Pupils can search for texts themselves that offer a good 'adaptation' and present them to classmates. They can research who owns the text, bringing in an understanding that stories can 'belong' to individuals and companies. This idea can be further developed by considering sequels, which are not owned in quite the same way. If *Rocky* can have four (or was it five?) 'sequels', what about a sequel to *To Kill a Mocking Bird* or *Of Mice and Men*? Pupils can check library resources to select a novel to 'sequelize'. In groups, acting as film producers looking for the right sequel, they will consider its appropriate market, the audience it will appeal to, and the operating knowledge such an audience might have.

It is highly likely that future classes working on the concept of adaptation will have available several current adaptations from the cinemas, on video or on television or radio. Linked to some of these adaptations will be numerous artefacts; Disney produces thousands of objects and advertising franchises with each new film. 'Classic' texts may provide only minimal promotional material and a new edition of the 'original'. Both ends of the scale will reveal strong evidence of the economic impact that the text is expected to make. Pupils can examine the artefacts to consider what they reveal about marketing generally but also more specifically for how this 'version' of the story has been made concrete through figures and objects. They might speculate on how an adaptation which has not been marketed in this way might be developed. What would be appropriate merchandise to accompany a cartoon version of *Oliver Twist* or a Hollywood production of *Emma*? Could the way an adaptation has been realized lead to another written version of the novel, an updating for example? Emma Thompson touches on this briefly in her *Diaries*:

> We discussed the 'novelisation' question. This is where the studio pays someone to novelise my script and sell it as 'Sense

and Sensibility'. I've said if this happens I will hang myself. Revolting notion. Beyond revolting.

(Thompson: 1996, 16)

It is likely that many English teachers will also find the concept revolting. However, in this example, pupils may find it useful to consider the interrelationship between Thompson's use of US money to finance her film and the studio's expectations of using her to make a profit. A novelization of *Sense and Sensibility* would certainly be a mutant text! But there are many forms of text, say a cartoon version of *Macbeth* that keeps the original words, which are much more of a challenge to simplistic prejudices of the elitist kind. For pupils, one of the key points is that this kind of work requires them to draw on and reflect about their textual knowledge. A great deal of such thinking can be speculative, combining a degree of analysis with creative ideas.

Adaptations can have a very interesting facet in that they also dramatize physical landscape in a very literal sense; this may be true of other moving image texts that are not adaptations but, in effect, audiences seem especially fascinated with the visual setting of an existing story. For example, the British television adaptation of George Eliot's *Middlemarch* was filmed in a small English town called Stamford and not in its 'real' setting of Coventry. Since filming, the number of visitors to the town has increased dramatically and these visitors have come to 'see' Middlemarch (Rice and Saunders: 1996). The appearance of *Brideshead Revisited* on American television generated a huge interest in the landscape and settings of the series, leading to the reproduction of Sebastian Flyte's bear Aloysius by a leading American designer. These two details – one a setting, the other a key artefact – open up rich possibilities to pupils for reflection on ideas about culture and heritage and identity. Investigating how a particular period is evident in films of Dickens's or Austen's novels or, equally, in *The Color Purple* or *To Kill a Mocking Bird*, leads to an analysis of key artefacts that are redolent with meaning for modern audiences. Pupils can also think about texts that might be set in *their* location. If a certain text was going to be filmed in their area or neighbourhood, what degree of artifice would be needed to make the setting convincing in terms of the necessary atmosphere? Or, how would the text have to change to fit the landscape? These activities draw very precisely on pupils' textual knowledge, both print and visual, and ask them to interrelate and to 'materialize' their ideas.

England is full of commercialized literary habitats and marketed landscapes such as 'Hardy Country' and 'Shakespeare's Country', all of which provide excellent scope for analysis. Stoneman's book on the Brontës (Stoneman: 1996) offers a fascinating account of how the Bradford-based British Wool Marketing Board, when planning to advertise its products in Japan, based its presentations on *Wuthering Heights*. Museum staff from the Brontë Museum worked with the Board to produce *The Romance of Wool*, a musical spectacle based on Heathcliff and Cathy (Stoneman: 1996, 217). Pupils can research the commercial potential of authors with local connections and develop some innovative 'uses' for these connections.

Pupils are growing up in a world in which cultural heritage is an extraordinarily complex concept. To some extent it has become a much more obviously capitalist enterprise with all the associated elements of workers, production, marketing, 'exploitation' and so on. But equally, it is providing employment and careers to many people and opportunities for local areas to celebrate their history. The example of 'Hardy Country' is a powerful one. His novels look set to be regularly adapted as moving image texts, and to some extent these are likely to be challenged by Hardy's remarkably atmospheric rendering of place. This imaginative quality is both a 'gift' and an entrapping stereotype. Pupils should have opportunities to reflect on the notion of cultural heritage from this economic and social perspective. It would be interesting to speculate on what Hardy currently contributes to the economy and why foreign visitors are so interested to see the 'real' places that Hardy used in his work. Pupils can analyse the advantages and disadvantages of living in a landscape which has such cultural 'value'.

This raises the possibility of pupils investigating adaptation as a global and intercultural phenomenon. A very rich learning environment might involve linking two classes from different parts of the world who jointly consider an adapted text such as the late 1990s film of *Romeo and Juliet*. A class from Australia and a class from England might compare their views of the Shakespeare play and consider how this 'American' version had affected their thinking. They then might speculate on what contemporary Australian or English versions of *Romeo and Juliet* would be like. A class from China and a class from Holland might identify the most popular soap opera style programme in their culture and exchange videos (via the internet) of a 'typical' episode. Each class must subsequently explain what they feel transpires in this 'foreign' soap opera, asking the other class for help when needed. Finally, both classes might speculate on whether the particular soap opera scenario could be adapted to the other culture.

So far we have not considered what seems the most obvious starting point for the classroom, which is the comparison of a scene in the 'original' with a scene in the adaptation. This is an extremely rich vein and will receive due attention in the next chapter, where some of the focus is on film language and concepts. In this chapter it is important to stress that such comparative work can be very successfully undertaken without too much concern about what might be perceived as 'technical' knowledge. Such work might be considered as at rather different conceptual levels.

At the simplest level, many pupils will have had the experience of seeing a film version of a text they have read and will have encountered some of the complicated reactions that were outlined in Thompson's (1996) schema above; and certainly the teacher will have a store of such experiences. Any teacher, when approaching work on an adaptation, might find it extremely useful just to activate the prior knowledge of the class in relation to their own 'visualizations'. Perhaps just posing the questions 'What is an adaptation?' and then 'What makes a good adaptation?' can lead to an exploratory discussion guided by the teacher. Pupils may well feel they lack knowledge and so some investigation can be devised using library resources but more likely the internet, for example looking at Film Education or The British Film Institute. Another simple but focused activity is to ask pupils to 'find' some adaptations by visiting their local video shop and/or by scanning the TV guides, particularly satellite and cable schedules, for titles where the little accompanying 'blurb' reveals the source of the adaptation itself. The teacher might tie all this in with the fact that they are aware that a 'big' new adaptation of a well-known text is coming up on mainstream television. Such an event is always surrounded by a complex set of interrelated factors such as advertisements, interviews with the 'stars', accompanying documentaries and even interviews with the adapter, a rare moment in the spotlight.

A rare moment of high profile can occur, such as in the autumn of 2002 when the BBC scheduled Andrew Davies' adaptation of

Daniel Deronda to be shown at the same time as Davies' adaptation of *Doctor Zhivago*. This created real public and media attention and eventually ITV moved its showing to another evening. By asking pupils to think through how this could have happened, this example might be used with pupils to discuss the prestige factor attached to the serialization of 'classic' texts. In a more general way it can help them to understand the whole issue of ratings and audience that dominates much of television scheduling.

All the above activities activate pupils' prior knowledge and also stimulate and extend their thinking and act as a preparation for a more focused and intensive period of work. So far, a range of examples has been used above of reasonably well-known adapted texts, but this approach will be avoided here as it asks too much of the reader who may or may not have read and/or seen a particular text. In this section it is much more the nature of the pedagogy that counts rather than any specific text. For many teachers the use of an opening scene will be especially effective for a piece of close comparison. The great majority of novels and plays have a very clearly constructed opening scene (or scenes) in which the author establishes a number of important elements. A class can read and consider such an opening and then work on how it might be 'realized' by a director. At the simplest level this might be approached almost as translation. For example we have met a key character, how has 'it' been described and how can that be translated into appearance, costume and demeanour? Which current 'star' would be suited to this role? Equally, we have a clear setting; how might that be created? Or, where might we set this to achieve the desired effects? Pupils might literally sketch out some visual possibilities, perhaps using some drama techniques to embody their ideas. The teacher can then bring in one or more versions of the opening scene(s) for the class to compare to their own visualizations; for this level of work the more 'faithful' kind of adaptation is best suited. Classic-type television serials are especially concerned chiefly to translate, as opposed to transform, such opening scenes and therefore make useful examples. This provides an excellent opportunity for close viewing and for analysing actual frames of film and also for even closer reading as pupils go back to the initial text to locate visual and other details present (or absent) in the filmic scene.

A further stage can be developed if one version of such an opening is more transformative and can be shown subsequently. This provides a greater level of challenge as the issue of interpretation comes to the fore. It can be connected to the points above about mutation and so the class can consider why the story is being retold in this deliberately different way and what it might suggest about the preoccupations of the film-makers and their implied audience. Equally, it can place emphasis on the notion of creativity; what is being added to the text; what is new about this interpretation; what you (the pupil) might do to create your own version of this opening moment. This last idea might then take pupils back to their 'faithful' versions and to the 'original' and then on to very deliberate attempts to be creative using all the symbolic resources they have encountered so far. Pupils will now be ready to use film language in order to express their creativity: this is the subject of Chapter 3.

Looking ahead

This chapter has tried to develop a comprehensive argument for a radical shift of emphasis in English teaching and to demonstrate that print is, in a sense, being realigned alongside other kinds of text. However, this realignment in no way reduces the educational importance of literature texts though it will change their status. This concentration on adaptations has shown how powerful and dynamic are the relationships between texts from different media. The proliferation of adaptations is not accidental; texts are being changed both by direct human agency and through the influence of much larger and longer term societal pressures. The one constant element remains our insatiable desire for texts.

English teachers have always been, in a sense, evangelical, seeing themselves as missionaries, determined to help pupils appreciate the special qualities found in the 'best' literature. However noble, this approach tends to put off many pupils and also implies that there are two types of reader: those who have been 'saved', and the rest who choose to read from the popular cultural texts proliferating in the world. This division is now made untenable in our transition to what needs to be a more liberal and sophisticated model of literacy. Teachers and pupils alike enjoy a wide range of texts from the simplest to the most complex; their interests are converging. We can all enjoy being knowledgeable about texts and consider that knowledge together in the classroom. Adaptations dramatize that convergence and offer wonderful opportunities for the teachers' literary and historical knowledge to enhance the developing textual understanding of pupils, whether they would ever choose 'classic' texts for themselves or not.

Adapting remains the key concept. Texts, so apparently object-like and static, evolve and adapt even as we pick them up and turn a page or turn them on. English teachers themselves can recognize where change is inevitable and inescapable. The proliferation of adaptations helps pupils to see the remarkable energy and staying power of texts, especially some 'classics'. Like other species, texts survive and show no signs of imminent extinction; in fact they interbreed and produce fascinating adaptation 'hybrids'.

Chapter 3

Teaching film

For a teacher interested in working with the moving image, perhaps the jewel in the crown has to be 'film', arguably the most important textual form of the twentieth century and perhaps the one cultural form that all elements in society share as a common interest. Even for those for whom film is not a personal interest, or for parents who simply buy the tickets, the medium has an encompassing societal presence. With such popularity and status comes a considerable degree of responsibility for educators and this chapter aims to provide a series of approaches that teachers can adapt and enjoy.

Chapter 1 put forward the case for the moving image to become a central part of English teaching, and in doing so discussed film to some extent and noted that it has its own distinct disciplinary history. Back in the 1970s the first qualification available to school pupils that focused on the moving image was indeed film studies. Although Media Studies is now far and away the most popular field in which the moving image plays a significant role, there are still many degree courses that include the word 'film' and there are many vocational courses, of which film 'schools' are a powerful component. In that sense film does not need English teaching but English teaching can only benefit from incorporating film into its scope.

Certainly it is worth reiterating that there has been a relatively recent renaissance in relation to film and education. The British Film Institute (BFI), having been a very powerful advocate, since the inception of the National Curriculum in 1989, for the very broad-based notion of Media Education, in the late 1990s took a much more focused role about the moving image generally, but giving chief importance to film; a return, some might argue, to its proper roots. The publication by the BFI in 1999 of *Making Movies*

Matter is a key moment, followed up in 2000 by *Moving Images in the Classroom*. The first text has not been very influential on teachers as yet, but it was (and is) significant nevertheless. It will be referred to a number of times in this chapter but here considered for what it symbolizes. This sharpening of focus is clearly much more important than some remote policy issue; the attention to film education is going to help English teachers very directly and practically and needs contextualizing if they are to take full advantage of the related benefits to their practice.

In 1998 the Department for Culture, Media and Sport (DCMS) asked the BFI to convene a working group to draw up a film education strategy, having already convened its own Film Policy Review Group which had reported that the British film audience is less adventurous than some of its counterparts abroad and that it should be a longer-term goal to create a more cine-literate population through education, in its widest sense at all ages and levels (DCMS: 1998, 6.7). By 'cine-literacy' it meant a 'greater awareness of the sheer variety of films on offer and a deeper appreciation of the richness of different types of cinematic experience, which would encourage more people to enjoy to the full this major element of our culture'. This seems much more about the concept of free-spending consumers than actual literacy, and a close reading of the DCMS report makes it very clear that its chief concern is about creating a bigger and more successful British film industry. In itself there is nothing wrong with such an aspiration and it is good news indirectly for teachers. As stressed in Chapter 1, this recognition of the economic importance of the moving image is the most determining factor in the appearance of the phrase in *Curriculum 2000* (DfES: 2000).

The momentum from the DCMS report led directly to the production of *Making Movies Matter* and subsequently to *Moving Images in the Classroom*. Whatever the economic drive of this chain of events, the BFI has recognized that it has a renewed opportunity to influence both educational policy and practice and it has, quite sensibly, seized this opportunity, not just in producing documents but in other ways such as research and development projects with real sustainable potential. At the same time the other key agency, Film Education, continues to provide schools with a constant stream of free, well-produced resources linked to current films and appears to have good and sustainable funding. There is unfortunately relatively little evidence of the extent of use of its materials or their impact on pupils' learning.

This renaissance suggests two important things. First, the emphasis on film *per se* is a very good one for English teachers who might now look forward to the genuine study of full-length film texts and to a curriculum that will help them develop pupils' capacities to undertake such work. Second, and perhaps paradoxically, it will encourage them to recognize that the film industry is as voracious of its consumers as any other and to consider that their own definition of cine-literacy may have a decidedly more critical edge than the bland and somewhat disingenuous one offered by the DCMS above. In fact, with older pupils, an analysis of some of the DCMS rhetoric would make a very valuable exercise in terms of both media and linguistic understanding.

This latter point leads to a final quotation, at this point, from *Making Movies Matter*. The BFI has very little evidence on which to base any of its recommendations about moving image teaching generally or even film work specifically. It comments on Ofsted's Section 10 Inspections as follows:

> The standard inspections of schools are not required to consider media education except insofar as it is part of English, and there is some anecdotal evidence to suggest that teachers will avoid using moving image texts during inspections. Such inspection evidence as there is – for example in an Ofsted report specifically on English in 1998 – suggests that the quality of work is limited and stresses the lack of progression in learning. Pupils will be set similar tasks at different age levels and the outcomes tend to be much the same. This judgement is much the same as that of an internal report by HMI in 1988, which expressed concern about the lack of learning progression, and is reflected today in teachers' uncertainty about what the appropriate levels of challenge and learning outcomes are at different ages. For example, a third of the BFI's 1998 sample did not feel confident in assessing pupils' media learning.
>
> (BFI: 1999, 33)

The comment about the 'anecdotal evidence' reveals that to teachers at present teaching film is a risk and you certainly do not take chances in front of Ofsted. Equally teachers lack enough experience of working with pupils on moving image texts such as film to develop a sound practitioner's sense of how to diagnose pupils' knowledge and to design developmental tasks. However, the time to take such an experimental approach has finally arrived and there is growing evidence of the very positive benefits on pupils' learning, particularly their literacy, when such an approach is taken (see below). English teachers have a long record as innovators; the conditions are increasingly ripe for them to make teaching film one of their key developmental areas.

Film: some working definitions

In writing this chapter for teachers the key issue is to achieve a balance between bringing in some very useful and relevant technical information and avoiding writing a substandard 'Introduction to Film': there are plenty of useful books already available for that purpose (Dick (2002) and Phillips (2002) are recommended). The focus needs to be on educating about film and on engaging pupils' motivation and interest to help them understand and enjoy it, even more than they do already. This chapter therefore points the reader towards much more comprehensive resources in case they might be needed. Each aspect of film discussed will be illustrated with a specific practical example of classroom application; the latter part of the chapter will review longer term considerations, putting the specific examples into context.

The term 'film' is perhaps in itself no longer particularly useful nor literally even accurate, as many films are made using a composite of techniques and digital video is increasingly important. However, we will use the term 'film' in two ways: first to consider it as a physical entity with certain properties and then as an umbrella term for myriad sub-terms.

Film is a material with properties, and this materiality is important. A number of effects with which young people are very familiar are made possible by the nature of film. It is important to examine film as a signifying element rather than absolutely as a physical/chemical phenomenon. For pupils, the essential point is what film can do and to understand how it does what it can do.

A useful starting concept is the fact that film is in itself a diverse and versatile material. 'Film stock', as it is known, essentially has a base that has a perforated edge: the base can vary in width, i.e. gauge; the most commonly used is 35mm. On top of the base is the emulsion which contains millions of light-sensitive grains: this is usually overlaid with a hard coating to protect it. The stock can be slow, needing more light to develop but then providing a very sharp image, or fast: fast stock, because it needs less light, is more usable in 'natural' settings, and is the favourite of documentary makers. The sound track is literally added to the film, usually on the very edge or even squeezed between the perforations. Finally, film is made up of frames, which, when projected at a certain speed, become invisible and create the famous illusion of the movies.

There is already plenty of material here to help develop pupils' understanding. Grasping the concept of the frame is fundamental to any film work, whether analytical or creative; video provides the simplest way to illustrate this with the pause button, because any pause reveals a frame. Equally, a 'still' offers enormous potential for analysing how films are constructed. In terms of film grammar the frame can be considered a basic unit of meaning although it contains many others within it. The concept of the frame needs more careful explication (see below).

Pupils can very readily understand the idea of film as a capture of light by looking at one or two examples and then considering the consequential effects on the viewer. A good way forward is simply to use an example of documentary footage and of more normal film and to ask pupils to describe the 'look' of the two texts: the teacher might want to introduce the term 'grainy' as a way of helping the group differentiate. The pupils are likely to move towards notions of realism. Documentary and news footage is not as sharp as a movie; paradoxically, this makes the images seem more real because we associate reality with news in particular. This leads very readily into discussing the construction of reality by different kinds of film. If a director wants to make us believe this is for real, what kind of film would be chosen? Equally, older films look 'old', allowing contemporary directors to create notions of the past tense within a story.

Colour

These simple ideas about the nature of film in a physical sense can be easily extended and developed by considerations of colour. Many modern films control colour through either lighting or lens filters (see below), but more atmospheric effects are achieved by opting for saturated or desaturated colour. Saturation essentially means 'flooded' with colour, so the atmosphere would be vivid and bright;

psychologically we tend to associate this with positive feelings. Desaturation is when a director deliberately 'drains' the scenes of colour, producing a grey/blue effect which looks cold and melancholy, very effective for creating a bleak and cheerless feeling. These are relatively simple techniques and pupils can readily appreciate their effectiveness after viewing one or two examples and can apply the idea to their own work or might be asked to consider one or two scenes from a book or play and to consider how colour or lack of it might 'set the right mood' for the scene.

Discussion of colour as an 'atmosphere' can lead to consideration of its symbolic value. Colour is always a powerful signifier; at its simplest in Western cinema at least, white is used for purity and innocence and black for evil and villainy, usually made emblematic through what characters wear in key scenes. These colours can also be used deliberately, ironically or satirically, or as 'disguise'. This kind of focus begins to lead pupils to understand more fully the crafted nature of film both as a complete text and in relation to the construction of shots and scenes.

Lenses

Equally, some consideration of the camera and its lenses will help pupils to articulate explicitly what they have learned implicitly. Any camera can have a filter over the lens that immediately creates an atmospheric effect in much the same way as the idea of saturation. Much more important for pupils is the need to grasp the use of wide-angle, normal, and telephoto lenses.

Normal is, as it suggests, the lens that feels to the viewer most like their natural perspective. Figures in the foreground look close but not too close and if there is some perspective to the background, things look distant and less clear. The wide-angle lens (sometimes called the fish-eye when used in close-ups) 'feels' unnatural. It makes everything look far away and also gives a 'deep focus' as all aspects of the shot, including the edges and the background, are clear and sharp; movement in relation to the camera seems unnaturally fast. In a close-up, the image is distorted and objects are curved, especially towards the edges of the shot; this creates a very intense, often surreal image, very effective in creating a sense of anxiety and danger but equally powerful for comic and satirical moments.

Just as 'unnatural', but perceptually without feeling so, is the tele-photo lens. This is the lens that 'zooms' in on a key figure. As it does so, an individual or an object comes into sharp but shallow focus so that we see 'it' very clearly but anything even a slight distance away goes 'out of focus'. We can thus see the movement of our key figure very clearly but other movements, for example behind her, look hazy and it is hard to judge distances so that when someone else enters the same plane as the key figure it appears sudden and can be very dramatic. The human eye cannot do this but it feels more 'natural' because it is the equivalent psychologically to focusing our attention. Typically we are attending to one key feature of our natural scene. So, if our key figure is walking towards us across the car park our eyes are on her movements and we are less aware of what is going on beside us or in the distance behind her but everything is actually still in focus. This lens gives enormous scope for directing our attention and for creating very rapid changes of focus within any shot; this will be discussed below.

Pupils will be given a basic understanding of how a lens works in Science, but no English teacher is likely to rely on this very strongly as children's resolute ability to resist transferring knowledge from one subject to another remains as consistent as ever. Almost any film will provide some very clear examples of the various lenses in action, although a 'guess the lens' type of approach is a somewhat arid methodology. It is more effective to engage pupils in a predictive mode, so choosing an action or strongly plotted film will help; this approach also draws usefully on pupils' regular use of predictive strategies in reading print, particularly narrative. The teacher can then stop the film at a key moment and ask pupils to predict what happens and to suggest what the director will do to visualize the scene. This approach is best combined with parallel work on shots so that the pupils are working out what the camera is doing generally and using a range of more technical terms to describe specific moments. The lesson might focus therefore on the idea of 'camera work' rather than just the use of the lens.

Light and dark

The other most basic ingredient in film is light and its absence. This can be achieved through uses of saturation and lens filter, but most of the time it is achieved through actual choices of lighting from 'natural' through to the full battery of lights used on a set. That most famous of all cinema phrases, 'Lights, camera, action', reminds us of the fact that in the history of the moving image the use of lights on an interior set is the dominant mode. It is worth reminding readers that the origins of the word 'photography' are 'graph' meaning writing and 'photo' meaning light, hence 'writing with light'; in telephoto, the 'tele' means across a distance. English teachers are likely to enjoy exploring some of these etymological issues with their classes. Lighting is a versatile resource, providing everything from the most dramatic to the most subtle of effects. As we shall consider later when considering pupils' own practical work, it is also far more important than most viewers ever appreciate, and partly explains why so many pupils find their own work so disappointing: the amateur 'look' is often principally simply a lack of artificial light.

The influence of light on our perception of the meaning of a moving image is easily demonstrated. 'Hard' lighting on a subject's face shows up that face vividly; the bright illumination reveals every detail, especially any imperfections; all shadows have sharp edges so that wrinkles, for example, are suddenly much more noticeable. 'Soft' lighting makes a face look much smoother and shadows become blurred and faint, wrinkles can disappear. These two effects are achieved essentially by 'hard' lighting being typically a single spot trained directly on the face whereas the soft effect comes from reflecting the source of light onto the face. Again our perceptions of the natural world are important here. We are used to the phenomenon of harsh lighting, particularly brilliant sunshine, but in such light we simply squint; objects, even faces, dazzle us. The only way to get the spotlight effect in the natural world is if light shines through some kind of frame like a literal window frame, striking and illuminating the figure being viewed. This effect is often used in the movies, appearing 'naturally' but simultaneously symbolically to 'light up' a character in a revealing way. However, soft light is a relatively natural phenomenon, most familiar to all of us at evening as dusk 'falls'; there is a period when the light of the sky, just after sunset, softens; the same is true just before dawn and sunrise. Movie makers frequently exploit this natural light to create atmosphere, especially in the more clichéd romantic movies.

Lighting might be considered one of the key vocabularies of the moving image and especially of film. It always conveys meaning and, because it has been in use for such a long time, it can almost be used as a kind of 'shorthand' for an audience. For example, a key character in a film might be soft-lit in a close-up and so she will look at her best; she answers a brief phone call but we do not hear what is said, then we see her face in close-up in a very hard light and we immediately know that she has had bad news and that this news has radically affected her feelings for the worse. Viewers are so 'used' to this that they are immediately clear about the meaning expressed but its artificial construction often escapes them. It is a key example of where direct teaching, using examples, can change their conceptual understanding of film and deepen their appreciation of its subtlety and its art.

Lighting is used in such myriad ways in film that it is beyond the scope of this chapter to do it justice. However, there are relatively few basic techniques and pupils should definitely be taught them so that they have a vocabulary themselves to talk knowledgeably about moving image texts. We will concentrate here, for simplicity's sake, on the face in close-up and the effects that lighting creates. Back lighting illuminates from behind, casting the face in shadow which may suggest menace but also ambiguity as we 'feel the need' to see the face properly. Bottom lighting creates the effect beloved by small children using a torch shining under their chins of looking menacing and somewhat ugly; this is a regular shot in the horror genre. Top lighting, if used by itself, is also unflattering, casting shadows under the eyes suggesting difficulty and perhaps weariness. Side lighting has a somewhat intriguing effect as it illuminates quite strongly but also creates many shadows, making a face harder to 'read'.

Obviously all of these effects can be made much more subtle once other light sources are introduced and also depending on where they are placed. Even quite strong lighting is softened if placed at an angle to the face compared to the camera. Much of the time several lights will be used in combination. There may well be a strong 'key' light which gives the dominant meaning to the shot, but 'fill' light, i.e. soft, reflected or filtered light which 'fills' out the subject's face, may be used; some back lighting helps to give definition and separates the background and foreground, making the image more three-dimensional. This is usually called three-point lighting.

The absence of light is just as powerful as its presence. For example, a 'high-key lighting' floods a scene or a character's face with bright illumination whereas 'low-key' will immediately create a sense of mystery and possibly menace. A classic cinematic effect is to keep a character's face in shadow so as to disguise identity until a moment of revelation. More generally, shadow and low lighting can suggest many effects, essentially creating atmospheres that heighten tension and suspense.

Introducing these concepts and terms to pupils will allow them much more subtlety in their description and analysis of actual scenes and images. Much of this vocabulary is directly relevant to Drama, and it may be that colleagues use it in their work with pupils. Equally, a really good lesson can be planned around using the drama studio or main hall to demonstrate these effects by using the right kinds of lighting equipment. If pupils can capture some of the images of lit faces with a digital camera then they can very readily create photo stories of changing moods and feelings or add captions to images to reveal the character's thoughts. This kind of work could make an excellent shared project with Drama and possibly Art.

Shots and angles

Whereas the theatre and the cinema share many features in relation to lighting, one thing that distinguishes them is the position of the camera; however much actors move on stage, or their lighting changes, the audience remains fixed and so perspective is also fixed. The movies do not move only in terms of the illusion of continuous movement; they also constantly move our perspective. This form of movement is achieved initially through the director's choice of shots and then more subtly through final editing. A shot is the basic unit of a film, consisting of an uninterrupted sequence of film, anything from a single frame to many minutes in length, typically a matter of seconds. Shots can be divided broadly into three categories: one is distance, the second is angle, and the third relates to camera movement; all of these may be interrelated at times.

There are typically six types of shot related to distance. The extreme long shot is regularly used in film as the 'establishing shot'. In such a shot the scene itself is what the viewer notices, typically the surroundings, therefore establishing something like 'this is the city' or 'we are in the mountains'. The subject, perhaps the main character, may be present in the shot but we only really notice them later when the camera picks them out. This might be achieved by the next shot being a long shot so that the subject is now closer and still has the entire body visible; it is still some way off but now more distinguished from the scene. If we then move to a medium shot this tends to mean that the camera can no longer keep the whole body in the shot, so typically we get a waist-up image; this provides plenty of attention to the scene but the character is now very visible in terms of features, dress and expression. As soon as we move to a medium close-up the frame is filled by the subject, so typically this will become a head and shoulders shot and the surroundings will become merely background. If we then move to the classic close-up, our attention is on the character's face and expression as the face fills the entire frame and there is no background. An extreme close-up takes us to one of the main features of the face, for example to the character's eyes or lips.

Of all of these shots, the close-up and the extreme close-up are the most cinematic. Sitting in a cinema seeing a face fill the whole huge screen is an extraordinary moment and a moment only achievable in cinematic circumstances; we experience a character's face in vividly dramatic detail, enabling us to see it in ways that the natural eye can never manage. This intense scrutiny of the face is one reason why stage and cinema acting can be so different. On stage the face is only a detail to most of the audience, on screen it can be utterly dominating and therefore the slightest change can be fully registered by the cinema audience. An understanding of this difference is especially important for pupils' practical work and may well be best taught by looking at 'close-up' shots from film and then asking pupils to recreate or adapt them using either a still or video camera; high-resolution digital cameras can also be very effectively employed.

The camera can adopt any angle in relation to the subject but there are four basic positions. The low angle 'looks up' at the subject, making it loom large and powerful; the effect of a monster is regularly achieved by beginning at its feet and then slowly looking up at the monstrous height and substance of the creature itself. High-angle shots look down on the subject, making them look potentially small and helpless. An eye-level angle shot places the camera at the eye level of the subject, so the camera is several feet off the ground to create the illusion of a kind of equality between subject and viewer or to let the subject address us directly as if we are 'there'. The bird's-eye view is the most dramatic. We are all familiar with looking down from a great height, but most bird's-eye shots are more deliberately disturbing than that naturalistic notion. For example, we can look directly down on a person as if they were literally below us, or we can look down into a room or prison cell in order to appreciate its size and shape, something quite different to 'normal' experience. With a helicopter bird's-eye shot we may follow a figure or a vehicle across a landscape. A less common angle is the Dutch, in which the camera is deliberately at a slant, so making the subject look as if they are on an awkwardly slanted surface; typically this angle either makes the audience feel disoriented or suggests that the subject's state of mind is disturbed.

For teachers interested to take this kind of analysis much further either for themselves or for their advanced students, the work of Kress and Van Leeuwen (see for example Kress and Van Leeuwen (1996)) is especially relevant. They have been working for many years on an extended project to develop a visual grammar, i.e. a way of explaining everything that has been constructed as a visual image in all its features and details. Just as linguistic grammar attempts to explain every aspect of language down to the minutest element, so visual grammar attempts the same for images. Inevitably, this is an extraordinarily complex task and requires an equally complex vocabulary. Most pupils are likely to find its complexities arcane and potentially bewildering. However, good teachers will find ways to help pupils think about the commonalities between a still image and a moving image scene where, for example, a similar visual technique is used in each. The use of a low-angle shot might be found in a poster, a magazine advertisement, a newspaper photograph and a scene from a film just to enable a class to see that there is a kind of visual grammar at work. Pupils might be asked to assemble a series of images over time to build up a mini-exhibition to demonstrate aspects of visual grammar to the whole class. There are excellent opportunities here to collaborate with Art departments to produce a joint outcome.

Visual grammar undoubtedly has great potential value for educators, but it brings to the classroom some of the well-known problems of linguistic grammar. It can seem abstract, highly technical and, to many pupils, not very beneficial to their understanding. This chapter has already reviewed a good deal of technical-sounding vocabulary in relation to film, and unless there is a great deal more emphasis on visual education throughout the curriculum from an early age it seems that we are already pushing at the boundaries for most teachers and their pupils.

So, to return to angles in film. So far all of these angles have been directed towards the subject, but the point-of-view shot is at least as important. In one sense we become the subject and see the events through her eyes. This is achieved by the camera first showing us the subject's face and that she is clearly looking at something, then the object of her gaze, then the next shot may be of the object from the position that we know the subject occupies. This places us in the subject's point of view but also may help to construct that point of view; for example, if the object is a soft-lit face in slow motion we may gather that the viewer is gazing longingly and lovingly at her and so we have understood the nature of the view. The point-of-view shot can also be used to make us feel we are directly in the scene, becoming the killer's victim or the killer himself and thus witnessing horrific scenes in the most vivid way possible. The point-of-view shot will be very familiar to pupils but will need explicit teaching to give them the vocabulary with which to describe and interpret its use.

Moving the camera

The camera itself can be moved in many ways. In the early years of the cinema, cameras were large, bulky and awkward to move so most technical innovations were about ways of moving the camera, for example on tracks and cranes; these techniques are still very much in use. More recently cameras have become lightweight and portable and so can literally be hand-held. With digital technology cameras can be very small indeed and no longer even need 'film'.

A simple but crucial feature is the tilting or panning of the camera. On a typically tripod-mounted camera such movements are smooth and controlled so that movement does not draw attention to itself. A simple tilt might be used to reveal a character by staring at her feet and moving up the body to humorous or alluring effect. The movement to the side – panning – allows the director to take in a large visual sweep perhaps a landscape in a slow steady motion, establishing a sense of atmosphere and space. Tilting and panning can be achieved simultaneously, for example, to move diagonally up a building or down a mountain scene. Panning can be used in more self-conscious ways, such as panning in a complete circle so providing a kind of panorama of the scene. A deliberately rapid pan, a 'swish' pan, creates a blurred effect and can add a sense of confusion and tension to a scene.

The camera being moved creates very different effects. Placing the camera on a crane allows movement through three-dimensional space, up over a crowd for example, or swooping down towards a key event. Equally, giving the camera wheels (a dolly) or putting it on tracks in various ways, allow the camera to move with the action or move towards or back from what is happening. An obvious example is when the director wants us to walk with two characters who are walking and talking, giving us a sense that we are naturally with them as they move. Both crane and wheel movements are predicated on the smoothness of the movement so that we concentrate not on the movement but on the subject we are concerned with. These techniques provide directors with enormous versatility and a huge range of potential shots.

The smoothness of motion of the camera was once almost a byword for professionalism of a film, shakiness being the sign of the amateur, rather like the out-of-focus amateur family snap. However, the advent of the hand-held camera has also extended the versatility of what the director can select. A hand-held or, more accurately, shoulder-held camera can be held very still, but equally it can be moved as the camera operator moves, creating a more naturalistic feel. Some directors also prefer the hand-held approach because the cameras are small and can be very close to the actors without much technical apparatus, creating an intimate feel; Woody Allen uses this technique in many of his films.

These highly portable cameras were not really developed for this cinematic purpose but much more to allow news teams to take cameras to the action zones of wars and disasters or, more ordinarily, to any location, however mundane or extraordinary. Cinema makers can thus incorporate the hand-held element when they want to create a sense of contemporary realism, perhaps for a part of the film. In recent cinematic history, *The Blair Witch Project* exploited the whole idea that hand-held/amateur camera work gives an authentic feel to the 'reality' of what is happening. There is a downside to this mobility, which is that shaky camera work becomes uncomfortable to watch and viewers can experience genuine nausea, rather like sea sickness, if they are susceptible.

The 'steadicam' is a relatively new piece of kit that provides excellent mobility but avoids all the disturbing effects caused by the jitteriness of the hand-held. The steadicam is a combination of a frame, perhaps best described as a kind of harness, which is strapped to the camera operator and holds a camera, a monitor and a torsion arm. This allows the operator to walk along and look at the monitor (not through the lens) and to adjust the camera's focus and direction while doing so: an operator can have all the smoothness of tracking while being able to walk up and down steps, in and out of a crowd and so on. As pupils gain some technical vocabulary, but more importantly understanding of the moving image, they can draw on it in their discussions and analyses of scenes and films whenever relevant. This suggests, as argued in Chapter 1, that an English department will need to incorporate moving image work in each year's curriculum to provide consolidation and sustainable progression.

Digital cinematography

The computer has transformed much of the work of the film industry, most spectacularly in the field of animation. We will return to this area more fully in Chapters 5 and 6. In relation to film itself, the creation of *Toy Story* as a totally computer-generated animation feature film in 1995 marked a key moment in this revolution. However, for most directors the computer is another piece of cunning to use in creating the illusion of film. 'Morphing', for example, allows for the image to be adapted so that one character is transformed into another. Equally, digital editing allows for details to be changed, for example an anachronistic detail in a period film can be edited out without any loss to the film's look. There is no doubt that in the area of special effects the computer offers enormous potential to enhance the vision of a director. Blockbuster-type films, the likes of *Titanic* or *Lord of the Rings*, can now create moments of extraordinary spectacle that no longer require a huge set and casts of thousands; both can be created using computer modelling. However, the new technology is still at the stage of enhancing rather than replacing what is already in use. The advent of DVD technology in the home may well lead to a different kind of revolution where some of the most dramatic effects of the digital kind are watched on the small screens of the computer and/or the television. Cinema may retain more of its traditional approach because of the social experience that it offers for the big-screen audience.

Editing

Most films are made up from the most traditional building blocks of all dramas, the scene. The scene itself is composed of a number of shots put together to create the scene, and editing these will be at least as important as the original filming. At the simplest level, at least where real humans are involved, scenes are acted and therefore may need several takes before they are properly realized. This will provide the director with raw material from which to construct an ideal scene made up from the best shots.

These days most pupils are entirely familiar in one limited way with the concept of editing through the proliferation of 'out-takes' often shown at the end of the film itself and, even in the case of *Toy Story 2*, a computer-constructed film that therefore could not have human out-takes, created as a postmodern play on the growing tradition of out-taking. This form of familiarity is certainly not understanding and may perhaps lead pupils to overly simplistic concepts about film.

It needs to be accepted that 'editing' is a difficult concept to teach. English teachers already know that helping pupils to be editors of their own writing is a huge task even though they emphasize it all the time and it is a genuinely practical activity, i.e. pupils can really practise. Very few schools can offer direct experience of filmmaking and editing, although the advance in computer technology is making this an increasing possibility: this is considered below and in more depth in Chapter 5.

The most successful way for the majority of teachers to help pupils understand editing, at least to some extent, will be through analysis of and reflection on existing film. Out-takes can act as a fun introduction but it might be better to use them as a fun conclusion to a lesson, as they are more of a distraction than an aid to thoughtful discussion. The ultimate aim is to enable pupils to understand what is, in essence, the most obvious point about film: that nothing is accidental in any scene of a carefully constructed film. This 'perfection' of construction is achieved through all the planning and preparation that goes into each scene and then the editing and 'post production' work that follows. Essentially, we want pupils to be able to discuss the *mise-en-scène* of any scene in a knowledgeable and informed way.

Much might be said about this French phrase, perhaps best translated broadly as 'staging', which also provides a sense of its theatrical origins and why it is now a slightly awkward term. It puts the emphasis on everything that is literally placed in front of the camera to make up the scene. Its value as a term remains in its emphasis on the artistic composition of the scene by the director and all the technical staff at work as well as the actors, so *mise-en-scène* includes the scenery, the lighting and so on. However, it can be slightly misleading in that a scene is a carefully selected number of shots; much of this work is done in the editing room. Again, pupils may have familiarity with terms like the 'director's cut' version of a film, i.e. a version released which is different to the original because the latter was edited down under pressure from the studio and commercial concerns. In other words, pupils will have a sense that any film they see is a selection from various versions usually of a much longer proto-film. But such understandings are very vague and 'director's cuts' are the stuff beloved of film buffs although a comparison of two versions can be a valuable exercise, especially for older pupils; the advent of the DVD is likely to be a valuable aid in such work as it has sufficient storage space to include more than one version of a complete film.

Helping pupils appreciate *mise-en-scène* must be through close viewing of scenes and through analysis at the level of the shot, drawing on the basic terminology covered earlier in the chapter. An extended example of an approach illustrates this, and here, unusually in this book, a particular filmic example will be needed to illustrate some key points.

Danny, The Champion of the World, adapted from the Roald Dahl novel, directed by Gavin Millar in 1989, provides excellent scope for the kind of work outlined above. First readers will need a brief but not exhaustive summary of the opening scenes and credits in order to give some concrete examples to discuss below. The production was a joint one between Walt Disney Productions/WonderWorks/Children's Film & Television Foundation/Portobello Pictures/Thames Television and this appears on the screen; the words 'Portobello Films' appear on the screen as if hand-drawn. The first scene consists of a number of rapid shots depicting men in traditional shooting clothes firing double-barrelled shotguns at pheasants; other shots are of the pheasants falling from the sky and dogs picking them up and carrying them to the shooters. There is no music, only the sounds of guns firing and birds thudding to the ground. The editing is very rapid so that each shot is no longer than a couple of seconds and is immediately followed by another; the effect is very jarring and disturbing.

The scene dissolves to black and a new scene appears of the English countryside looking at its most charmingly picturesque, accompanied by jolly 1950s film music of the Ealing Studio tradition. The camera pans slowly across the landscape as the year '1955' appears, followed by 'Somewhere in England'. Over the next few minutes the names of the chief actors and director etc. appear. The camera comes to rest on a picturesque long shot of the countryside. In the distance is a small wooden building (this turns out to be the garage where Danny lives, but we do not know that at this stage). The scene changes to a country park with thousands of pheasants and the camera very slowly pans past a large tree and comes to rest on a long shot of a large country house that fills the frame. In the foreground is the drive leading up to the house; as the camera rests on this image of the house, the title *Danny, The Champion of the World* appears with fanfare music; the typography used for the words of the title is 1950s comic-book style and very colourful, in contrast to the plain white lettering used for the credits. We hear a door slam; the shot changes to a medium close-up of a man (Mr Hazel, played by Robbie Coltrane) in slightly ridiculous country squire clothes and the music becomes sinister and deliberately villainous. He looks at the pheasants and we realize (point of view) that he owns and covets them in some particular way.

The rest of the credits are played out as we see him enter his Rolls-Royce, drive through his estate, meet two of his gamekeepers and then drive across the country to a field where there is a sign, 'Hazel Estates'. He gets out and looks down at the building through his binoculars – 'we' see through these as he brings into focus the building and we can just see a car and a small figure beside it. The shot switches to a low-angle, extreme close-up of a 1950s car and its petrol cap; the camera pulls back and slowly up, to reveal the car, a small boy (Danny, played by Sam Irons, the son of Jeremy who plays his father) in overalls, then the petrol pump, then the forecourt, then the whole, wooden and slightly scruffy garage. We hear a few words in the background and then see an old gentleman coming across the courtyard (the doctor played by Cyril Cusack, Jeremy Irons' real-life father-in-law). Danny cheerily explains that he has filled the car up. The next few shots are alternates of scenes at the garage and of Hazel racing down the hill in his car, until he hurtles into the garage yard and almost collides with the car that Danny is backing out of the garage. Danny's father emerges at the same moment as Mr Hazel gets out and the latter tries to persuade Danny's father to sell him his garage.

This is, in the best sense for teaching, a very obvious text and ideal for developing pupils' film vocabulary and understanding. One way to open up the text is to divide the class into smallish working groups of three or four and to give one of three tasks to each group. Task one is to note text of any kind; task two to note all sound, and task three to note shots; as the third task is most difficult it is best to advise these groups more carefully. The class as a whole can be given as much context and information as the teacher feels will help, and the class will definitely need to see the whole sequence twice and to try to refine their notes and ideas as they do so. Technical vocabulary can be introduced before the tasks are undertaken, between the two viewings or at opportunistic moments at the teacher's discretion.

The opening text giving information about the financial backers and film-makers offers opportunities to discuss the concept of film categories and institutions. The film is very clearly an expensive (scenery, costumes, authentic details, well-known and reputable character actors) family film with international appeal and definitely with an American market; this leads to discussion of the stereotypical, chocolate-box depiction of England for a US audience. The stars of the film are classic British actors and some of them are even related. The typography of the title and of 'Portobello Films' prompts consideration of the significance of how text looks as well as what it says. The precise year, contrasted with the emblematically vague 'Somewhere in England', provides an interesting insight into the symbolic status of the story as somehow representing something about 'England'. The estate sign prompts discussion of the use of text as information within the setting.

The opening scenes use sound very directly. The first scene has no sound, a most unusual approach in itself helping to alert pupils to this fact. The music shifts from comic-book 'jolly' to comic-book 'villain', always then directing our attention and shaping our response to the images on screen, helping pupils to see how integral sound is to our understanding of the moving image. There are several simple and specific deliberate uses of sound. The discordant and abrupt bangs and thumps of the opening sequence are very noticeable and provide an excellent pointer to the dark side of the story in counterpoint to the sunny pastoral scenery. When Hazel closes his front door it bangs, echoing the sounds of the guns; the same happens with his car door which sends pheasants scurrying and hurrying away. His Rolls-Royce is always accompanied by screeching tyres as he goes round corners, or whooshing sounds as he hurtles down country lanes. Each of these sound effects is important because their distinctiveness helps pupils to appreciate the constructedness of the sound track (for example, Rolls-Royce tyres do not screech at 20 miles an hour). Equally, each of these sounds helps build our understanding of Hazel's character as a loud and brutish bully.

The opening shots are all short, in harsh, bleak light and jump-cut to create an almost bewildering collage of carnage among the pheasants. The fade to black neatly signals the end of the opening sequence and offers a symbolic interpretation of the destruction of the pheasants. This is then very deliberately contrasted with a soft-lit landscape and slow, mostly panning, movements across gorgeous, sunny countryside. The opening shots in this section include a slow dissolve, slow pan, medium close-ups, close-ups of faces and objects, long shots, a helicopter bird's-eye shot of Hazel's car looking like a nasty black beetle crossing the landscape (this shot also has the cinematographer's credit).

Two other sequences offer excellent discussion points. The first has Hazel sitting in his car smoking a cigar. Two of his men (clearly real ordinary country people dressed in simple, appropriate and authentic clothes) approach, tip their caps and say 'Morning sir'. He (rudely) ignores them and says nothing, throws the cigar onto the grass (close-up shot) and drives off. The men watch and (medium close-up) shake their heads in disapproval, a neat example of a reaction shot telling us how Hazel is perceived by real country people. The second has Hazel in the field scene mentioned above. He looks down at the garage, makes a kind of 'humph' sound as he focuses his binoculars; the sound is a kind of animal, guttural noise suggesting his possessive, acquisitive nature. We then see his point of view as he 'looks' through the binoculars (we see through two circular shapes) and we zoom down to the garage and see the little figure by the car. This zoom shot (not possible with binoculars made in the 1950s that can only focus, not zoom) provides a clear example of both point of view and also the construction of meaning as the director, using the camera's telephoto lens, literally directs us to the hero, Danny.

Finally, these shots help to prompt discussion of editing itself. Hazel is up on the hill and the little figure we see is not distinct. As the camera pulls back from the petrol cap, revealing Danny, we 'make' the connection that this is the same figure, but we are now down at the garage so at a different location and at the beginning of a new scene. The editing gives the illusion of a continuous flow of narrative, joining up the story for the audience. The camera angle stays low, giving us the child's point of view throughout most of the scene. Now the shots are alternately of the garage where this location is established or of Hazel hurtling down the hill, showing pupils how parallel editing gives the audience a sense of stories happening simultaneously and almost certainly having a connection to be revealed, as indeed this does as the two cars almost crash and so, symbolically, do the characters. The conflicting parties are now established for the audience.

After this level of close attention it is now possible for the class to reflect at both micro and macro levels. For example, why did the director start with the shooting scene when it might seem more logical to begin with Hazel or with Danny? This very short sequence can be reviewed to reveal how entirely the effect is created by the editing of a number of shots in rapid succession and by the absence of music and the intensity of the sound effects. This prompts discussion about the themes of the film and about narrative cohesion of the whole text. Why is there no music in the opening scene and then music of the period of the film rather than of the period when the film has been made? What does the style of music and style of typography for the title suggest about the nature of the film and the way the narrative will be 'told'?

Finally, this film is a very typical adaptation. At one level it is very faithful, using the basic idea of the story, the main characters and working hard to evoke the 1950s English setting. However, in other ways it takes great 'liberties' with the text in order to create what is an effective cinematic text. There is plenty of scope for discussion about this should the class read the whole book and view the complete film. However, some points can be developed just using the opening section described above. For example, the openings of the book and film are quite different and this might be explored. A few pages into the book there is a brief physical description of Hazel which is a model for the film character, and this might be analysed in relation to the first shots of the 'villain' in the film.

Teachers will select their own texts for classroom use but it has been necessary here to examine one 'real' example in some detail just to suggest the richness of such work and particularly to illustrate how cinematic terms and concepts like editing can be taught. However, even with this level of detail about Danny, a great deal of further potential work has inevitably been left out. The scope of teaching film in the English classroom is enormous and will feature again in Chapter 7, where the emphasis is on the future.

Chapter 4

Making the most of television

Chapter 1 discussed the relative decline of teaching about television (in school settings) over the past 20 years, and this chapter begins by examining some of the issues related to this decline. When the medium achieved its period of dominance, arguably from the late 1960s through to the early 1990s, it received regular attention in the English classroom, perhaps most intensely in the 1970s and early 1980s when video unlocked the potential of television for classroom use and when the BBC and ITV were heavily committed to producing high-quality programmes to support teachers' work. During the 1980s, in particular, there was some excellent work to produce programmes to support the major changes in English brought about by the introduction of the first 'common' examination, the GCSE and its very different emphases, for example making speaking and listening a high priority and an assessment focus. Equally, the move to make literature more accessible, but also to conceptualize it much more broadly, led to the production of some outstanding programmes. These all still exist and may well 'return' in digital form as the television stations continue to recognise the extraordinary value of their archives.

During this period television was equally prevalent as a topic in itself and as a generator of topics. In the former case, many English teachers were interested to discuss with their pupils the issues about the influence and impact of television on society and young people in particular. The depiction of violence on television was a consistently controversial and important topic. Television was equally important to English teachers as a stimulus to the consideration of topical issues for debate and discussion; nuclear power, for example, was a regular focus for classroom exchange and there was always something to prompt such work on the news or in documentary or fictional form.

The first key point then, is that teaching about television has had an important and valuable role in English teaching and there is a body of work about such activity that remains central to teachers' development, as discussed below. However, as for example Hart and Hicks' recent research suggested (Hart and Hicks: 2002), television now features relatively rarely in English teaching. Part of this can be explained first by the increasing curricular prescriptions of the past decade or so and then, even more draconian in effect, because of the National Literacy Strategy and its emphasis on print. It is not without irony that the dominating collections of videos in most schools are tapes of classrooms where model lessons of the literacy hour variety are demonstrated; the training video may be English teachers' most regular viewing? Another part of the explanation relates almost certainly to the increasing prominence of the computer. Although computers are not yet themselves very regular components of English lessons, there is clear evidence (Ofsted: 2001) that teachers are more likely to devote any 'screen' time to PCs rather than TVs. This does appropriately reflect some societal changes, particularly the increasing presence of the computer in young people's domestic settings. Finally, television, partly as a result of the rapid growth of the internet, has lost its status as chief media villain. Essentially television has been upstaged by controversies about computer games, internet pornography, chat rooms and so on and these are, of course, absolutely important issues.

However, in beginning now to put forward the case for television to be central to the English classroom, an initial point relates exactly to recent media panics about computers and especially the internet. That point is that comic books of the 1950s had their own dominant time as the chief corrupting influence of their period, followed by rock and roll, followed by television and so on. Now television has become so ordinary, so everyday, that we are in danger of neglecting its central importance to the culture of all our lives. There clearly is a danger that the pedagogic expertise developed by English teachers will be even further diminished unless something is done. This is reinforced by the evidence considered in Chapter 3 about the renaissance around film, especially the educational resources being concentrated to 'make movies matter' by the likes of the BFI and Film Education. So a paradox emerges that just as the moving image finally appears in the official curriculum and appears to have some political backing, so the technology which still dominates the production and consumption of the moving image may be absurdly neglected.

Partly as a result of this paradox, the importance of television in teachers' thinking cannot be taken for granted. There is an urgent case both to restate the rationale developed by educators in the 1970s and 1980s, and to reshape that case for a digital age and for a model of multimedia literacy and for a time in which the nature of television viewing has radically altered and will continue to evolve.

What we already know about television and education

The genuine relationship between television and formal education has always been complex while often portrayed quite simplistically. For English teachers the relationship has been, and still is, characterized by this complexity and also ambivalence. We do 'know' that television has been, and still is, a vast source of information and of entertainment, and this means that English teachers enjoy and value the medium for themselves and for their pupils as consumers, but are often suspicious of television's seductive power to influence and to entrap young viewers with 'trash'. This is actually more of a creative tension than a serious problem.

The basic argument for taking television 'seriously' as an English teacher, developed in the 1970s and 1980s, exemplifies this creative tension and can be conceptualized as the 'first phase' of such teaching. Research had revealed that the original conception of television as a kind of monolithic dominating force directly affecting an undifferentiated mass audience was simply untenable. As soon as viewers had choices between channels and programmes they made them, and producers soon discovered that they could not 'control' and reliably keep an audience. For teachers, one key element in this conceptual shift was the change in awareness about children's relationship to 'the box'. Much early 'conservative' angst had been about the susceptibility of the innocent child to this super-powerful new medium and this remains a tradition, mostly in right-wing cultural criticism. Texts such as *The plug-in-drug* (Winn: 1977), *Amusing Ourselves to Death* (Postman: 1985), *A is for Ox: The Collapse of Literacy and the Rise of Violence in an Electronic Age* (Sanders: 1995) continue to argue that television is essentially the equivalent of a debilitating mind drug and demand that it be banned from settings where it can reach young people. As suggested above, English teachers do have some sympathy with this view. This sympathy partly derives from their inherited position as cultural mediators. The great majority of English teachers have been formed within the literary tradition of great books and this carries with it a great deal of cultural baggage. Eagleton (1983) has argued that all English teachers are Leavisites whether they know it or not. In other words, their instinct is to be suspicious of the popular in any form and to evangelize the 'great' texts. This is an oversimplification but it is a real element in teachers' thinking and it can be a real problem in relation to television. Whereas film, as argued in Chapter 3, has a long 'respectable' history as an art form, television is rarely accorded high status; in fact this rarity exemplifies the issue, suggesting as it does that an exceptionally 'good' television programme goes against the general rule. In order to help pupils understand television, English teachers have to recognize this literary tradition as essentially a kind of handicap, a set of blinkers.

Equally, English teachers have always been interested by the question of displacement, that is, what children might be doing if they were not watching television, particularly whether they would read more books. The Benton survey of children's reading and viewing habits (Benton: 1996) produced some interesting findings. There are children who relentlessly watch television and read nothing, but they are in a minority. Most children moving into adolescence watch many hours of television in a week and, as they get older, read less. This seems useful evidence for suggesting that the study of television gets progressively more important, especially as young people watch more and more adult programmes over their adolescent years.

Recent research (Livingstone: 2002) emphasizes the way technological change is affecting young people's television consumption among a range of interactions with other technologies. This is one factor in what we need to consider as the second phase of teaching about television. One key change is the move to multi-set homes. Although the 'living' room still contains the 'main' television, many teenagers and often much younger children have their own TV and VCR and their viewing is not very restricted by parental control. This is by no means universal but it is certainly a relatively common phenomenon and one recognized by adolescents themselves. An important element in the multi-set home is the distinction between the television being 'on' and it being 'watched'. Radio has increasingly been categorized as a background medium, i.e. the radio might be on in several rooms with no-one apparently paying it attention. This phenomenon appears to be increasingly true of television, and especially so for adolescents with a set in the bedroom. This phenomenon may help teachers to think about their potential role as teaching viewing in quite an explicit way.

The other fundamental change in the second phase is the multiplicity of choice. In the 1950s homes had one black and white television with one channel, in the 1960s some homes had colour and two channels, in the 1970s there were three channels and video allowed for time-shift viewing, so for the first three decades of television viewing in the UK, change, looked at retrospectively, was slow. The culture of television was also very conservative, with the essential model being the BBC's public broadcasting/paternalistic concept of 'proper' service to the public. In the past ten years or so, and very rapidly in the last five, there has been a revolution in provision and certainly a shift in culture. Provision now includes hundreds of channels offering everything from the recycled mainstream to very niche subjects which will only ever attract a small audience; it also includes a rapidly developing level of interactivity which has its own range from the shopping channel concept to pay per view. The postmodern viewer is often characterized as the 'zapper', endlessly roaming the channels in search of a few minutes' interest. This can be seen as yet more evidence of the mindlessness of the passive consumer, with the proverbial gnat's attention span. However, it is equally possible to see this as the ideal discriminator who can, for example, avoid every commercial by simply skipping them. Inevitably, the typical viewer (and pupil) seems to be a mixture of such characteristics. This is part of a new culture of television and is partly a result of a different culture of consumer. This hybrid culture is very commercial, but the consumer can be far more demanding and 'discriminating'. The range of choice is huge, yet the viewer may watch far more selectively, no longer suffering the tyranny of the bland mainstream.

Television remains and will remain a hugely important medium. Its proliferation through cable and satellite broadcasting, the constant creation of more and more channels, its constant inventiveness of new programming formats and its increasing interactivity suggest it will remain a dominant medium for the foreseeable future. The English teacher's approach to teaching about television needs to draw on the pioneering work of the first phase and to be fully informed by the creative opportunities of the second.

Still soap opera after all these years

Soap operas remain a phenomenal success. Beginning on radio back in the 1930s and sponsored by soap powder producers interested in capturing the female consumer, a genre was created that appears to be infinitely variable and yet very consistently characterized across the globe. It can be argued that soap opera is actually only a relatively recent variation on the timeless human need for hearing stories about people, from the trivialities of gossip to the devastations of tragedy. In the domain of print there have been very comparable genres, and almost any serialized story form has similarities to soap opera. English teachers might usefully reflect on the 'high art' of writers like Dickens who wrote for the public in episodic serial form, whose crafting of cliffhanger endings kept the public in genuine suspense and who would have been entirely comfortable in being called 'popular'. In most cultures soap opera appears to work against the fragmentations of postmodern viewing by retaining a hold over large, multi-generational audiences and by making this audience 'share' the lives of the characters and their unfolding stories to the extent that they are a feature of 'real' everyday life, read about and talked about by a kind of community of viewers. Soap opera also illustrates especially clearly how the social science (Media Studies) perspective and the artistic (humanities/literary) perspective can jointly illuminate and enrich classroom work.

The term 'soap opera' is somewhat loose and certainly needs some scrutiny. The following discussion is intended to be culturally specific to British soaps, although most Australian ones would also fit. To 'fit' in the soap opera category a programme will tend to be characterized by having several showings per week, therefore fitting in with the 'everydayness' of life. It will usually be shown before actual 'prime time' and this will include the afternoon and very early evening. Episodes will be relatively short, typically 30 minutes with occasionally 'long' or 'special' programmes to provide a little (but definitely not too much) variety. The programme concept will be of a single, geographically very specific setting featuring a community focused around easily identifiable setting locations, some social (the pub, the café) and some featuring the relatively private spaces of key families. There will be no 'main' character or hero/

heroine; instead there will be a considerable number of key characters whose current prominence will be determined by one of the featured narratives that usually last for many weeks, often months. In British and Australian soaps the people must be 'ordinary' and much of their lives must exude the mundane, but at the same time they will experience constant drama and frequently melodrama. Characters are often emblematically good or bad, especially the latter; every community must have its likeable rogues but also some genuinely nasty villains. The latter point is true of American prime-time soaps, but in contrast there the stakes will be much higher financially, with great fortunes always to be made and also lost.

This definition, helped with a little use of cultural comparison, is certainly a good starting point for pupils. The issue is not what they watch or how often but what knowledge and understanding they have of the genre; this takes the more social science approach and helps to keep the personal and favourites etc. out of the classroom discussion. The teacher can engage a class by helping them develop a tentative definition which is then tested against the example of several of the best-known programmes. Comparisons with examples from another culture can help to sharpen the definition and also enable pupils to 'see' that there is a culture at work in such texts. The representation of minorities or 'different', e.g. gay, characters is always highly revealing (see below).

The other dimension associated with British soaps is that they are also ordinary and mundane in the sense that they look and 'feel' inexpensive. Production costs can be relatively low and satires of soap operas always exploit this 'cheapness' to easy comic effect by making scenery fall over or by having deliberately poor camerawork and so on. Pupils do need to think about the relentless production schedules involved in producing two or even three hours of programmes every week, keeping the stories up to date through references to current events and weaving in topical issues. The production team therefore has to use the same studio sets all the time and the actors have to learn their lines almost continuously with shooting; the time for sophisticated editing is minimal. With constantly improving technology these practical constraints could be more frequently overcome than they are, but the 'ordinary' look is now more a part of the semiotic landscape of the soap than an absolute necessity; in other words the 'cheap' look is as much a style choice as a technical necessity. Pupils can be readily introduced to this key feature by just a few minutes' contrast between a British soap and a film or an American prime-time soap.

In order to focus from the huge range of possibilities concerning work on soap opera two examples will be offered, one aimed at a Year 8 age group and the second at Year 10, with one intention here being to illustrate opportunities for planned progression in moving image work and media education more generally. The emphasis in Year 8 is on character and setting, in Year 10 on soap as a phenomenon and as a television institution. In both cases, however, the class needs to be clear about the popularity and enduring appeal of soaps, although with Year 10 this has a greater importance. Pupils always 'know' how popular soaps are but they need to base this vague understanding in some more definite evidence.

For Year 8, work might begin by taking a simple look at the programme schedules on the five terrestrial channels for a week to identify when and where soaps appear. In order to do this the class can first develop the definition offered above and use it, tentatively, to include and exclude programmes. They can also hypothesize about when and where they expect to find the programmes before checking this out by a close reading of the schedules.

The main purpose is for pupils to appreciate the pervasiveness of soaps and also their particular timing within the schedules but not to go into great depth: that kind of focus is better suited to Year 10. It is generally helpful to focus on a soap which is well established such as *Coronation Street, Eastenders* or *Emmerdale*. It is important to watch an episode in class, partly, and obviously, to give the class a shared specific text to analyse but equally to avoid endless vague references to other episodes or soaps, a potentially negative feature of media work which distinguishes it from work on literature. The class can begin by watching the opening sequence twice and on the second viewing commenting on what expectations the images create; it is especially effective to turn the sound off so that there is no longer a comfortable familiarity with the opening. The opening of soaps typically locates the particular series in a recognizably clear geographic location so the shots are panoramic or tracking shots revealing streets or countryside.

If there are pupils in the class with plenty of knowledge of the soap then this can be utilized at a later stage; initially the class needs to 'study' an episode. The class will work best in small groups, each one having to create family trees of the main character groups and a list of the settings with brief descriptions. The episode is best viewed in segments with each change of location triggering a pause for the groups to pool their observations and make notes. This approach is inevitably time-consuming and requires intense concentration, and may be usefully spread over two lessons.

Any episode will provide a useful range of the standard locations and of the majority of the characters. Having discussed the overall range of characters and locations with the whole class, it is then possible to consider what each of these features 'provides' within the soap. For example, which settings are 'public' and which 'private'? Which characters 'belong' to which settings and what do we learn about them from their setting? Characters will initially be considered by Year 8 pupils through their personal attributes. Small groups can be given a character who features in the episode to analyse in a character study, initially within the arts paradigm, i.e. how does he behave, what does she say about other characters, what attitudes does he reveal, what feelings does she show, etc.

This approach can then be developed by the group moving more into the social science paradigm and analysing the appearance of the character, particularly dress; what does the 'costume' and the assumed accent reveal about social status, for example? Is the character one with significant power in the soap? How is the camera used to help us follow the character's part in the story? This latter question should involve the group in reviewing part of the episode by themselves and picking out a key moment or two which they feel provides evidence for all their ideas about the character. This activity is also valuable in 'training' pupils in moving image analysis and in the idea that they need to 'study' images to interpret them. When appropriate each group can present a 'portrait' of their character and its significance. The whole class, with the teacher's guidance, may then be ready to consider the emblematic nature of the characters within the soap and how each location provides a kind of frame for viewers to 'recognize' and so interpret meaning.

This character and location work can be developed in many directions. Individual pupils can use their character as a basis for a traditional 'character study' or creative work in which the character tells the story through diary or letter form. Individuals or groups can do more media-related work by creating a new character group and setting and by providing a rationale for their introduction. Equally, pupils might work on identifying a current topical issue and by working out a story line and deciding which character or characters would be best suited as 'vehicles' for the story.

Work of this kind in Year 8 provides a solid basis for a more sophisticated analysis in Year 10, especially if moving image work is a feature at some point in every Year's curriculum. It is important explicitly to reactivate the group's prior knowledge and previous work by revisiting the definition of soap opera and by analysing their place in the schedules. If there has been no previous work on soap then this stage acts as an introduction to the study of soap opera (see above).

Concepts such as 'institutions', 'ideology' and 'representation', the bread and butter of Media Studies, are rarely considered in English, yet their importance is fundamental. The study of soap opera (and news, see below) is ideal territory for work on these concepts and, importantly, it is a territory where English teachers and pupils can meet with confidence. These concepts are not easy to 'teach' and so familiar ground can certainly help both teachers and pupils.

A good starting point is to examine soap opera as a 'phenomenon'. Once the class has established a working definition and a clear sense of the genre's prevalence, it becomes important for them to reflect on its significance. A good question is to move from 'what is it?' to 'what is it for?'. It is helpful to get the class (as far as possible) to put aside personal views, favourites and prejudices and to investigate the phenomenon and its enduring popularity. At an exploratory stage there are a number of avenues and the teacher might allocate different tasks as research or provide some input to the whole class on each aspect. For example, the genre has a history including the origin of the name and there are notable issues in the development of the genre, the success of *Coronation Street*, the launch and establishment of *Eastenders*, the failure of *Eldorado*, even the enduring existence of *The Archers* (the BBC Radio Four serial that is the longest running soap opera in the British media). In fact *The Archers* is a useful complement to work on moving image soaps because it offers that important 'defamiliarization' technique which can help pupils reflect more deeply on the nature of the genre, as listening to a soap is such a genuinely novel experience. *The Archers* can also be used to help pupils imagine how the scenes they hear, and therefore potentially visualize, might be realized on camera. Finally, *The Archers* has its own important place in soap opera history and pupils can benefit from an understanding of that point. Teachers themselves should not feel a need to undertake burdensome research; it is more important to help pupils see that for all their 'everydayness', soaps are long term and enduring and in that sense they have become a form of media institution.

Another useful avenue is to let pupils look at audience figures and then speculate on what that audience is composed of; for example, what is their personal knowledge of who watches a particular soap? Do the commercials before, during and after a soap reveal anything about the audience that the advertisers think watches the programme? Given the timing of the programme, who is at home to watch it? Again, given their personal knowledge, who makes time to regularly watch a soap? This personal knowledge can then be tested by looking for audience research or by investigation by the class of family and friends. The 'big' soaps have huge and remarkably loyal audiences, with a genuinely broad spectrum of society represented.

It is also valuable to explore the nature of the 'stories' in a soap. At any given time there will be several identifiable stories at different stages of development. It is a useful exercise to take two of the big soaps and ask the class to identify and then track a week's 'worth' of 'plots' and to try to explain their significance to the audience; a good question is something like 'what makes the writers include this story; who and what is it for?'. Some stories will clearly be the stuff of melodrama, someone's affair, the 'discovery' of someone's parentage or the 'consequences' for a character of some previous, often 'secret' action. One story, perhaps more, is likely to reflect some current or ongoing social issue: alcoholism, illiteracy, environmental concerns and so on. Having gathered the evidence of the stories, it is important then to ask the class to reflect on which stories will have been 'talked about' in the community of viewers and by whom in particular. This leads on to the opportunity for the class to move beyond the notion of the generic satisfactions offered by soaps to considering the notion of viewers as a community; that is, people for whom soaps are part of an identity, a facilitator of gossip and discussion about life and its problems, large and small.

These avenues should lead to a reasonable understanding of the nature of soap as a social phenomenon, i.e. some of its history, some of the 'appeal' to regular audiences, aspects of its structure and nature, its role in enabling a community of viewers. This groundwork can be a basis for tackling the concepts of ideology and representation.

The class should now be clear that a soap is a social construction meant to be representative of 'everyday life' while at the same time dramatizing that life even to frequent melodramas. But what exactly does it represent, and what are its 'values'? Academic research on soaps typically portrays them as strong transmitters of mainstream values (see Burton (2000)) and as especially powerful in participating in a culture of conformity. Therefore, the moral system is simple and based on a fairly crude 'crime and punishment' scenario whether in the personal/moral sphere or in the actual world of good and bad deeds. It is seen as reflecting some of society's residual values, for example adulterous women are especially likely to be punished with unhappiness; working class characters are essentially 'stuck' in that class and their attempts to leave it are doomed to failure. The other element frequently attracting critical comment is that minorities, when they are 'represented', are treated at best ambivalently. They can make for a good and melodramatic story about, say, the treatment of gays, but if a character or group becomes part of the 'regular' soap then they become subsumed and tokenized.

Such comments on soaps are recognition of their limitations but equally they identify exactly why they are so enduringly popular. Occasionally, a new programme will take a risk with the intention of capturing a new audience; this has been especially true of programmes making gay characters the central protagonists. However, these programmes deliberately have only some of the features of soap opera and play on the 'difference' between the characters' lives and those of 'normal' society.

It is especially challenging but particularly important to enable pupils to interrogate the ideology of soap opera. Even though many pupils may be enthusiastic viewers and may resent what they might perceive as an attack on 'their pleasure', there is an approach which can help to get beyond that perspective. In any soap there will be some 'young people' and even a few children but it is essentially an adult world, that being one reason why it appeals to pre-adult viewers. A useful lens for pupils which helps them focus on the ideology of soaps in a relatively objective way is to investigate what this adult world 'is like'. This also provides opportunities to analyse representation and stereotyping across the genre.

There are a number of ways to develop this critical analysis. The investigation of 'typical' characters is one approach, for example the 'role' of the barmaid or the 'downtrodden woman'. Equally valuable is the portrayal of a minority. Pupils first need to identify which group is apparently represented and then to build up a detailed account of them and of their interactions with the 'majority'. This approach can be complemented by asking pupils to test the soap boundaries. What kind of 'outsider' or minority figure could be introduced, and if so would they be a comic or serious figure; to what extent would they 'disturb' the norms of the community of the soap, both its characters and its audience? This kind of investigation is likely to reveal that the mainstream nature of the soap is powerful but not absolute; British soaps do introduce controversy. At one level this is simply about drama and about maintaining audience interest: part of the skill of the soap writers that pupils can appreciate. At another level it can be argued that the notion of mainstream is always self-contradictory and riven with paradox and that soaps are in that sense a helpful part of society's thinking aloud. Pupils can themselves think about this by considering whether soaps can 'shock' audiences or influence their thinking in any direct sense.

In Year 10 this kind of study of soap opera, and of its institutional status and its centrality to the institutions of both the media and society, should equip pupils to comment on soaps as a phenomenon. They should have an answer to questions such as 'What are soap operas for?'; 'What makes a soap opera successful?'; 'Do soap operas provide an important contribution to society?'. This section has given some idea of how soap opera can be studied in the English classroom, but it is only indicative of the richness of the material involved.

News and documentary

Whereas soap operas can undoubtedly claim to be popular and even significant in the lives of adolescents, most research suggests that news and documentary are marginal in every sense. Many pupils pick up bits of news from music/local radio and even from casual contact with newspapers, but this does not reflect any conscious or purposeful seeking of the news or current affairs. Indeed as Buckingham (1996) demonstrates, some young people actively dislike and avoid news because it overwhelms them: their response is essentially emotional; they cannot bear to watch the horrors of real life. This is an important and often neglected factor for teachers to consider and also emphasizes that news is at least as much drama as information. Equally, whereas young people might have encountered news because it did form a part of the ritual viewing in most households, now they may be in the seclusion of their bedroom with their own TV avoiding news altogether.

But adults certainly do value and consume news. An important aspect of the second phase (see above) for teachers is the sheer relentless availability of news. Some channels provide nothing else, 24 hours a day; this is perhaps taken to its logical extreme in North America with channels solely devoted to weather. The nature of news being produced in both a 24 hour culture and within the rhythm of the more 'normal' working day will be discussed below. The great majority of adults claim to watch news and to value it. It might be argued then that an interest in news is simply a feature of maturation and of accepting membership of the adult world: why not let this development happen 'naturally'?

However, it seems more important to point out that this 'naturalness' is part of a potential problem. It might be argued that soap operas, for all their conventionality, are actually more open and dialogic texts than the news, so often presented to us as 'the facts'. Television news is a very highly constructed genre and any emergent citizen needs to be able to get the most from it but also to read between its apparently seamless lines. Documentary, although equally constructed, is also vital because it remains one of the few aspects of television with any radical, even non-conformist, purpose. The news, in its widest sense, is too important to neglect. There is a danger in all this worthiness of losing sight of the fact that television also offers really alternative views of current events through its topical and satirical programmes devoted to humour. British television, in particular, has a long tradition of satire and parody that certainly has a powerful influence on the way viewers interpret current affairs and counterbalances the somewhat pompous and sanctimonious posturing of much traditional news broadcasting. Working with television news, in a broadly defined sense, can be fun as well as serious.

The genre of news

Television news is a highly stylized and conservative genre; within it there are interesting, even subtle, variations that can help pupils to decode its signs; for example the exact degree of formality of the presenter's dress and manner and, increasingly, physical position, standing or sitting, behind or in front of the 'desk'. Newscasters themselves can have a celebrity reputation and their 'appearance' outside the news 'box' can be revealing of their particular status.

For pupils a good starting place is to focus on a short but complete news broadcast, recorded to allow for intensive viewing and reviewing; ideally a major programme and time, for example an early evening BBC broadcast, provides the best material. Another useful hint is to avoid a day with any singularly important piece of news, as its dominance and undisputed prominence disrupts some of the more 'normal' conventions of the genre. It might be worth studying such a broadcast after pupils have familiarized themselves with a more typical and conventional broadcast.

As with almost any moving image text, the opening few seconds deserve close attention for their use of images, music (or sounds such as Big Ben) and for their iconographic features such as the lettering in titles, the way words and images move or are juxtaposed. Typically, the openings attempt to achieve a mixture of gravitas and drama, usually with some iconic references to the notion of panorama with images of the globe of earth, satellite imagery of identifiable countries and so on. Pupils need to see such a packed opening several times to decode the range of associations being made through image, sound and text.

Pupils always know enough about news to analyse the opening successfully and to have an implicit sense of appropriateness. So before showing the next establishing shot, pupils can work in groups to discuss their anticipation of what will happen next and how the presenter will be presented to the news audience i.e. dress, voice and 'the scenery' surrounding the news reader. They can then watch to see how accurate they have been. The next section of the broadcast always contains the establishment of the voice and face of 'the news' with the camera closing in to medium close-up, so that the backdrop is initially visible as is the physical positioning of the reader, still typically behind a desk, followed by a head-and-shoulders shot of the anchor person speaking the traditional formal 'good evening' or equivalent. Pupils need at least some of the language of film (see Chapter 3) to appreciate the way the shots are constructed and also to be able to describe the moment when the pre-recorded introduction gives way to the 'real' and 'live' news.

This notion of 'language of film' is a good focus for analysis. The pupils can consider what ingredients go into the 'ideal' newscaster;

for example, clothes, facial expression, 'props' (desk, notes, computer) and setting/scenery. They can contrast this with one or two other 'presenter' roles, for example sports reporters who will be broadly similar, although 'lighter' in some ways, and comedy hosts who will be typically very different. This idea of 'presentation' can also help pupils appreciate how, for all its formality, news is presented by characters who talk to 'us' intimately but seriously. The class might consider several other familiar greetings used by other presenters in 'live' situations ('How are you all doing this evening?', 'Are you having a good time?') to consider how the opening of the news and its voice position the audience into a respectful silence. We are invited to the spectacle of the news but we are not to interrupt.

One of the technical points about news is to help pupils appreciate how the newsreader can look straight at us all the time. This is because of the autocue, placed so that the reader can read while looking up; she is looking at words, not at us. Pupils can try writing a short item and reading it while 'looking up': they soon appreciate how impossible this is. This can also be contrasted with the way a comedy presenter working with a live audience will not look at the television audience, i.e. into the camera, much of the time but will do this occasionally and dramatically so as to include 'us' in an intimate and conspiratorial way at key moments; this 'look' is often at the expense of some hapless member of the audience or guest and gives 'us' an equivalent status to the presenter: something we are not offered by a newscaster. Pupils can also consider the role of the notes or computer that the presenter may have, what might be called the props of the news scene. They may or may not be used but clearly they add to the news scene by emphasizing its basis in information prepared for our benefit. The *mise-en-scène* concept from film is very valuable here (and for other analyses of television) because it allows pupils to consider the detailed construction of what is very much a set. This is equally true when the scene includes, typically as part of the backdrop, a 'glimpse' of the rest of the 'busy' newsroom, or a bank of computers, so that we are even more convinced that this is not only up-to-the minute but 'authentic' news.

The majority of broadcasts begin with the 'headline' tradition of newspapers and so mention the 'top story' and either go straight to that item or at least illustrate its importance with a shot or two of 'the situation', then highlight other key stories before launching into the main story in detail. A useful preliminary exercise involves taking the items from the news the day before, just expressed in the headline, and giving them to small groups, asking them to put them in the order in which they were presented. It may be helpful to include in this list the one story that is frequently used which is the 'light' story – the only one that involves a smile from the newscaster – so that pupils can identify its specific function. The main purpose of the exercise is to help pupils see how news is selected and to begin to understand how selection is in a sense the 'creation' of news. They can also attempt to categorize news items. Some terms seem relatively simple, political, scientific, environmental, criminal and so on, but pupils need to focus on the 'spin' of the story, drawing on more emotive words like scandal, shocking, dramatic, triumphant, celebratory, horror. The news presenter through a combination of words, tone and facial expression will position how we should react, 'Shocking news tonight . . .'; 'Another horrific outrage was perpetrated today by . . .'; 'A new scientific breakthrough promises to revolutionize . . .'. A great deal of this positioning is verbal and radio broadcasts can be used here to help pupils appreciate, by concentrating on the words and tone, how powerful are the linguistic and vocal emotional markers in the 'factual' news.

Television news will inevitably combine the linguistic with the visual, whether a still or moving image. An important, more general point here is television's obsession with filling the screen continuously. Even when a news item requires no image there will be one and there must never be a moment when we are 'in between' items, there must be seamless continuity, the audience must always be clear that to leave the screen is to miss something vital. Ironically this is a partial recognition, after years of audience research, that audiences rarely give their full attention to the screen. The illusion that they do must be maintained, especially during something so self-consciously important an 'event' as the news. Pupils can study this by identifying whenever a potential gap comes along, the end of an item within a programme such as a news broadcast or a magazine-style programme, the end of a complete programme, the commercial 'break', to build up a description of television flow; this can be done diagrammatically as well as in words. Pupils can also investigate how the link to the next or other programmes often comes before the end of the previous item: this is especially true with films which have the indulgent habit of listing everyone involved at the end, which can take several minutes of screen time; a voiceover typically comes in with a 'Don't go away because . . .' message. News programmes which include a commercial break use a similar technique by highlighting the importance of items in the second half. Observing these techniques and reflecting on them helps pupils to understand the concept of seamless flow and also television's, or more strictly each channel's, very particular obsession with maintaining its audience.

Having considered issues such as the context created to deliver news and the selection and creation of news, pupils can move on to analysing the intricate construction of news stories. News must always maintain its up-to-the minute dramatic style while simultaneously giving the audience a sense of considered objectivity, of purposeful news-gathering by reliable and trustworthy reporters. Pupils can examine the various interactions in a typical broadcast between the presenter (or presenters) and the other people and pre-prepared items. Before viewing the main body of the news broadcast, pupils can try to list what they expect the 'ingredients' will be and, with the teacher's help, identify some of the following: reporting 'live' from the scene, interviewing at the scene, reporting from outside a key location (the Houses of Parliament, Buckingham Palace), studio interview, a special (pre-filmed) report, extracts from a press conference, still image with voiceover (often used for court reports where filming is banned in the UK), use of archive footage, interviews with the 'man in the street'. For this more fine-grained analysis, pupils usually need much more help and direction and may need to have such analysis modelled explicitly for them.

Having worked in this way in class, and once the teacher feels that such knowledge is secure, pupils can become more independent. The following brief suggestions sketch out some ways that pupils might extend and deepen their understandings. In each case this might be done as a whole class, small group or individual project.

A challenging but important concept in media work is content analysis. When looking at newspapers or magazines this means literally measuring column inches, i.e. how much actual space is devoted to a story. This approach becomes much more powerful if done over time with the same media text or comparatively across texts that can legitimately be prepared, for example tabloid newspapers. With news broadcasts the same concept can apply but the quantitative measure is time and there must be some recognition of the length of the broadcast itself, so the time is judged as a percentage of the whole. Content analysis can be used in many ways. It can illuminate how a particular story can dominate but more importantly how certain kinds of news typically occupy more time: reports about celebrities, for example. It can also reveal aspects of representation; pupils can 'count' appearances and time on the news. As with soap opera (see above), when minorities feature, who appears in the story and for how long? How is their presence framed? Is it a positive or negative appearance? When items appear to include the public, as in 'man in the street' interviews, who gets to represent 'us' and why? Content analysis is very much the social science paradigm and it is time-consuming and painstaking and definitely not for the faint-hearted. However, pupils can undertake it independently over a period of time and it can produce very powerful data as the basis for an essay or a project.

News is constant and yet episodic. Pupils can look at the schedules and identify the 'hard' news programmes across a day or a week and look at when they appear and what they imply about people's lives and their ability to attend to news. They can compare news on two (or more) channels to identify whether news is just news or whether, for example, ITV and BBC actually have institutional differences in style or selection. Pupils can be helped here by adding radio into the research. It is very easy to distinguish between the light style of commercial radio's news broadcasts and the solemnities of the public sector, Radio Four in particular. Pupils can look at comparative features of the various news outputs to identify the generic features of news, partly discussed above: for example, analysing the opening sequence of the major bulletin of several channels to look at the use of theme music, sounds, image and text. This can be followed by looking at the top story and the other stories and comparing both treatment and selection of news. Pupils can investigate particular techniques and trace them across the channels, for example how 'key' interviews are used compared to 'man in the street', when filmed reports appear and why, what newscasters have in common, how 'from the scene' reporters appear and how they sound, how staple elements of the news such as 'victims', 'relatives of the affected', 'the disadvantaged' and so on are handled: the list of possibilities is endless. With 24 hour stations it is even possible (if the school can provide the opportunity) to watch news 'as it is happening' and to discuss what difference this makes but, more importantly, how much these apparently continuous programmes stick to the 'formula' of the serious episodic broadcast in order to give themselves viewer credibility. The contribution of the internet and its use of images, sound and text is an interesting and evolving medium for news in itself (see Chapter 6).

Generally pupils need a good deal of teacher input and well-selected material to get over their initial prejudices about the news. They also may have, as mentioned above, more emotional reservations about news and this point may need to be addressed directly. But any school serious about notions of citizenship must help pupils understand both the importance of news and also how the genre 'works', especially its constructedness and its ability to manufacture news itself. Once pupils have been given the conceptual tools to analyse news they are most definitely empowered and able to deconstruct it.

There is not space here to go much further, but this challenging and serious-minded work can lead on to pupils considering current affairs from other perspectives; indeed, teachers might deliberately include in the serious analysis of news some of the 'alternative' representations of news provided in formats such as satire and straight comedy. Some of the conventions of news are regularly used in satire and are very helpful to pupils because they must be absolutely recognizable to viewers; for example look and sound like the news anchor man, but also discrepant or divergent from the norm, for example by telling a joke about a politician. Pupils can articulate how this combination 'works'. If there are opportunities for practical work (see Chapter 5), pupils can try out aspects of news reading and reporting, both serious and comical, just through using one video camera and watching the results on the 'box'. If they have considered current affairs in this broader and more inclusive sense they can reflect on television itself much more widely, even to the extent of a genuine cultural analysis perspective. Such a perspective would ask some fundamental questions about the role of television in culture, particularly its generation and control of news and information. In a democracy, what controls, if any, should be placed on news? Can 'mainstream' news ever represent minority opinion or should there be an alternative number of broadcasts? Should news be more specific to an audience in other ways; for example, are the news-type programmes for children and young people useful or merely patronizing? In times of 'crisis', is news censorship justified?

Documentary

In this much briefer section, the idea of reporting and information is developed further by a consideration of documentary as a form. In some ways the two features of this chapter, soap opera and news, are brought together in some of the newer and hybrid forms of documentary. For example, terms such as 'docudrama', 'docusoap' and 'reality TV' have emerged as television has experimented with notions of the 'real' and everyday while maintaining its search for drama and entertainment. This hybridity can certainly offer a starting point for pupils as they analyse the schedules in search of that slippery concept 'realism'. It can be illuminating for a class to begin by looking for a range of 'subjects' and trying to categorize what they find. Pupils might look for some or all of programme elements such as 'real people', 'real places', real issues, true stories, analysis of important matters in depth, real and controversial topics, a reconstruction of reality, real events in real time (not pre-recorded or edited but 'live'), and so on. Initially, this is likely to produce a large number of programmes and some discussion about which programme belongs where; it can also be organized as a classroom activity with programme names on cards and with headed spaces to locate them.

Pupils will discover that the 'real' appears in many places and in many forms and that even in a news programme a 'dramatic reconstruction' may be used. They are likely to find that this unsettles their sense of what is real and true and to what extent they can trust such notions; this state of mind can be confusing as well as challenging and teachers need to move pupils on to a position where they can tolerate such uncertainties. Rather than starting with what might be called 'classic' documentary, pupils are likely to find it helpful to start by working on some of these more familiar forms of 'realism'.

A way in to documentary, particularly 'fly on the wall' style, is to introduce a camera into the classroom and suggest to the class that there be a collective attempt to film an ordinary and typical lesson. The camera, if on a tripod, needs to be in a very obvious and obtrusive place and to be moved during the lesson; if 'hand-held' the camera person will need to roam around filming close-ups of pupils 'at work'. The results can be watched by the class and compared to a current or recent docusoap, with the focus on considering how the 'normal' and real can be somehow maintained in front of a camera crew. The class can then discuss how a lesson could be filmed to create the illusion of normality. Ironically, the English department's collection of training videos may be of use here with pupils, who are expert in what classrooms are like, viewing some examples for their truth to life qualities. They will definitely be able to point out their constructed nature and may also be able to recognize the use of multiple cameras and therefore editing. The teacher may need to choose such an extract and to help pupils notice this especially important part of the illusion.

Essentially, this is all 'awareness raising' style work but it may be built on later if practical work (see below) is an option. The class can return to a consideration of the concept of documentary by a further consideration of docusoap, analysing much more closely this time for the techniques being used to create the sense of it 'really happening'. One feature they will notice is the use of voiceover to make viewers make sense of each incident. With teacher help they can also consider how editing is used to select the critical moments that make the documentary interesting and entertaining and also the creation of 'characters' that the audience can 'get to know'. Camera work is frequently used to create a sense of closeness with the characters and their situation and they frequently speak directly 'to us', the camera acting as our eyes and ears. Pupils can also consider how the kind of 'drama' we are offered is deliberately 'ordinary' in the way soap opera is 'ordinary', i.e. the selected melodramatic highlights of a community's life, not its long periods of mundane and routine activity that are the true stuff of the ordinary.

This leads on very effectively to a consideration of the more traditional role of documentary as a form, and one especially important and highly developed within television. Pupils may feel very comfortable and even knowledgeable about the hybrid forms of documentary considered above, but 'true' documentary is rarely watched by the majority of pupils except when it links with an interest such as sport or music and when the form is often disguised. Ironically, they may well have been exposed to a range of documentary programmes in school, as teachers from all subjects frequently use selections from mainstream programmes to support their subject teaching. For most of the time, however, pupils will not have registered the fact that they are watching documentary at all and may well claim never to have seen one.

The teacher is inevitably going to need examples of the form to allow pupils to develop an understanding of both what documentary is and also how it 'works'. Given the increase in televisual provision, even just on terrestrial channels that are now 24 hour, there has been a relative decline in what might be called straightforward documentary programming, partly because it has been replaced by the hybrids. There are some programmes on prime time but they tend to be of the flagship style, classic examples being natural history series of the David Attenborough type. They do offer some insights into the techniques of documentary but they are essentially what is increasingly called 'edutainment'. The focus is on 'showing' the viewers, for example, the natural wonders of the world and so helping them understand and appreciate them. There are entire channels now devoted to this concept, particularly for Geography and History, and with the advent of digital television this concept is likely to gain prominence and more variety in content. It is a factor which a class can consider in thinking about the provision of documentary on television, and might well be conducted under the umbrella of 'non-fiction'.

Some prime-time programmes retain the more hard-hitting edge of documentary because they are of the exposé type; these programmes offer pupils a chance to consider the notion of documentary as investigative and controversial. They will contain some elements derived from the documentary form, typically by focusing on the identification of an issue where there is a matter of an injustice and therefore where an investigation might reveal causes and even solutions. Such programmes tend to be morally simplistic and often set out to find a villain or villains and to 'catch' them in the act, leaving the viewers with a comfortable sense of justice being done and a neat narrative closure.

Documentary at its best goes much further than edutainment and is much more complex than quick and dirty exposé programmes. It can really challenge viewers' assumptions about an issue and can offer insights that very powerful institutions, governments in particular, are often keen to deny the public. It is perhaps best exemplified by *Panorama* and *Horizon* style programmes. Such programmes are often buried in the schedules outside prime time but reachable via the video recorder. All a teacher needs is one decent example of a serious-minded documentary with which to work.

It is worth pupils reflecting on the origin of the term 'documentary'. A 'document' for most people is an official piece of paper or report, but the Latin origin was a form of proof, with the implication of a kind of lesson, or even warning: the more modern association with a written artefact really comes from the development of writing as a reliable form of evidence. So, a documentary is much closer to the original meaning and an understanding of this notion is helpful to pupils in grasping its essential and distinctive purpose as a form. As so often with initial work on a media artefact, pupils can refine their thinking by hypothesizing about expectations. In this instance they might explore a list of terms and decide which they anticipate will be present in a documentary. The list relates to attributes: entertaining, informative, exciting, humorous, glamorous, serious, educational, controversial, objective, biased; the list could be longer.

Pupils ideally need to view a complete documentary, although the teacher will judge whether this viewing is best broken down into sections or whether any content is unsuitable for a particular class. Equally, if the learning outcome is more about documentary generically, a substantial section may be enough to illustrate key features such as the defining of the topic, the role of the key presenter and his/her serious relationship with the audience, the use of interviews, particularly with participants and with 'experts', the development of an argument, the build-up of a momentum in the investigation/revelation, and so on. Any good documentary is very likely to engage pupils with the topic itself and can act as a very strong stimulus to debate and discussion and to further research by pupils to seek evidence about the programme's claims.

Documentary is also one of the few forms that pupils can undertake as a practical project which retains some proximity to the professional format. Although in practical work process is often as important as product, there are times when it is valuable to give pupils some of the satisfaction of a well-made practical product. Making a documentary allows pupils to identify an important issue and to plan and execute creating a programme that investigates and analyses that issue for a real audience, for example fellow pupils, parents, even the local community. This will be more fully explored in the next chapter on practical work.

Conclusion

As suggested in the opening of the chapter, television is in real danger of becoming neglected by teachers but it remains far too important a medium to allow this to happen. An especially important point is that the vast majority of moving image experience that pupils have comes from television rather than film and this dominance will continue into adult life. This brief examination of a few aspects of television has attempted to illustrate at least some of the potential for the English classroom. The final chapter will return to the medium with more of an eye on the future and with further opportunities for English.

Chapter 5

Practical work

English teachers and 'the practical'

As 'practical work' is frequently considered problematic, this opening section examines English as a subject and initially reviews notions of the practical in a general sense. Such a review is vitally important because many English teachers have a great reluctance to undertake what they consider 'the practical'. Traditionally, this has been exemplified by the difference between the English teachers who genuinely 'do drama' and those who make very selective use of a few drama techniques in their classrooms and who would tend to teach a play as a static text. This polarization is, to some extent, an exaggeration but most teachers will certainly recognize this characterization as rooted in real classroom practice. Since the introduction of the National Curriculum in 1989, a number of factors have moved English teachers to undertake more Drama in the true sense of the word, and this will be of use in considering moving image work below.

The major element, therefore, has been the explicit emphasis on Drama within the National Curriculum, effectively making Drama teaching a requirement, not a choice. A rather more positive factor derives from a number of sources (teacher training, in-service courses, particular projects such as Shakespeare in schools) that have combined to influence teachers' thinking to a more genuine acceptance of Drama as part of an active learning pedagogy. However, there is an even greater reluctance to undertake any work which involves what might generally be called 'the technical'. For many teachers, (almost) mastering the video player was quite enough. Another reason, therefore, for examining the notion of the practical in English is to make it clear that English teachers can undertake moving image work in a variety of ways that are well within their current comfort zone. Later, some evidence will be provided of how the nature of the new technology becoming available to schools is making what used to be genuinely difficult technical operations effectively simple and very manageable.

Practically English

The notion of practical work in English is generally a confused one, and the term itself is not really part of the English teacher's vocabulary. This is not a pejorative comment. Schools themselves are victims of a long-running debate about what is, and is not, practical. Its most extreme version is the endless uncertainty about the need to reconcile the academic and the vocational because they are almost always conceptualized as in opposition: in schools the former has all the status and the latter has almost none. Within the teaching profession, the general view is that some subjects are essentially practical and others are not. Using the lens of this view, Design and Technology and Physical Education are practical whereas History and Mathematics are not. Indeed, the term 'a practical lesson' will be used within a subject such as Science to distinguish between what might be called the theory and the practice; this may be a more helpful way to work for pupils.

However, what is a subject like Drama? Is it 'very practical' and therefore especially suited to less academic pupils, or is it a very academic subject whose expression and language are to do with the physical as well as the cerebral? Inevitably to most practitioners it is a rich combination of both. It is also especially important to stress that Drama and practical media work, while offering an 'academic' experience where appropriate, have a very powerful appeal to both less able (in school terms) and disaffected pupils and students; this will be further explored below. Underlying much of the above conceptual exploration is a much cruder and more influential distinction between subjects in which pupils move about and use their bodies and those in which, in the peculiar ways schools operate, pupils chiefly sit still.

This latter distinction is a good starting point to reflect on English. Teachers already engage in what is essentially practical work on a regular and routine basis; they tend, however, not to conceptualize it in this way, so a case needs to be made. Firstly, pupils do move about in English, principally when activities are derived from or based on Drama and most typically when related to a dramatic text. Secondly, speaking and listening activities do essentially involve movement and speech even if the movement may be limited to facial and bodily gesture. However, this notion of the practical, which teachers might already accept, is not sufficient, especially when a consideration of media practical work is involved (see below).

In a chiefly unconscious way pupils are regularly involved in practical work. The example of writing makes this clear. First, this involves a 'doing' activity; writing is an excellent example of something that requires physical exercise (still true with a keyboard) and mental effort. Second, the pupil is engaged in making something. This element of production is made obvious when the outcome is a poem or a story; texts that have beginnings, middles and ends and have forms and shapes on the page and so on. These texts are made and remade and can be 'finished'. This is true of almost all texts produced in English but pupils', and usually teachers', real sense of this process of 'making' is much more acute and conscious. In speaking and listening, the notion of 'making a speech' also illustrates this point about producing, but the work of Britton (1970) and others established very clearly how much speaking is a working-out and trying-out of meaning and understanding. In other words, a great deal of speaking and listening in the classroom has a routine practical component.

In the history of the subject (see especially Peter Abbs' work (Abbs: 1982)) there is a long-standing tradition to make the English classroom more like a workshop or 'atelier' (see Ellis and Robinson (2000)) where the emphasis is on English as an expressive subject and where pupils constantly shape their own experiences into artistic meaning. This tradition is very inclusive of a range of activities that would include aspects of art, music and drama as the norm. However, although this tradition is present within both formal documents such as the National Curriculum and existing classroom practice, it is very much a minor element. It is generally seen as part of the unfairly maligned 'progressive movement' and lacking in academic rigour. Equally, it is positioned as an indulgent approach and not a vehicle for delivering the 'basics'. The rise to dominance of 'capital L' literacy (see Goodwyn (2002a), Ellis and Robinson (2000)) is the most significant example of this reaction to the alleged inadequacies of the child-centred approach to education.

In fact, whenever the word 'creative' appears it tends to divide educators into various and oppositional camps. For some, the process rather than product group, it is the key to a good education and they would argue that many more activities involve the creative dimension than is recognized; in English, for example, they would suggest that almost all writing contains a degree of creativity. Others, most notably the genre theorists (see for example Cope and Kalantzis (1993)), see discourse as the key to empowerment. In their view the world is dominated by a range of often competing discourses, some of which are immensely powerful; the educator's job is to teach these explicitly, leading eventually to pupils' mastery of a genre and therefore an ability to use it effectively. Another group is best called the functionalists. They do not rule out creativity but they first prioritize 'getting things right', the idea that without the basics there can be no real communicative capacity. They also share with the genre crew a deep suspicion of what they would consider the Romanticization of the creative child, an almost reverential belief in the capacity for originality of the artist, something which every child may have. Can there be a balance between these views, or are they part of a range of 'tools' in the Vygotskian sense of available modes of engaging the mind and learning (Lee and Smagorinsky: 2000)?

In English this debate has usually centred around writing (see Ellis and Robinson (2000)), media work rarely getting the prime focus for discussions of creativity. It is also reasonable to say that the versions of the English National Curriculum of the 1990s are predominantly a reading curriculum and that the Framework for English of the early twenty-first century continues this approach but with an even narrower emphasis on school-centric literacy (see Goodwyn (2002a)). There are contexts where ICT is employed, especially with multimedia capacities, when some of these boundaries simply dissolve (see Tweddle *et al.* (1997), Goodwyn (2000)); this will be discussed below and also in the next chapter. Overall then, English has become a much less creative learning environment for teachers and pupils and they repeatedly say so (Goodwyn: 2003). This paucity is surely a very strong argument for emphasizing the creative potential of practical moving image work and for seeing it as one area where genuine production is possible. However, we need to turn to thinking and arguments from Media Education and Media Studies to find a really developed rationale.

To some extent there has been a similar debate among media educators but its depth and range have been greater and its ability to refer to more genuine examples much more helpful; its suggestions to resolve some of the oppositions cited above are especially helpful to English teachers. The key review remains *Making Media: Practical Production in Media Education* (1995) by Buckingham *et al.*, partly because of its comprehensiveness but also because its focus is very frequently the English classroom. More recent, though smaller scale, studies are referenced below.

Learning from the experience of Media Education

What might surprise and also challenge English teachers' thinking is that hostility to practical work among influential media educators was very prevalent for a considerable period and still carries weight. Len Masterman was especially virulent in commenting on the use of video cameras in the 1970s, suggesting that it only produces 'an endless wilderness of dreary third-rate imitative "pop" shows, embarrassing video dramas, and derivative documentaries courageously condemning war or poverty, much of it condoned by teachers to whom technique is all and the medium the only message' (Masterman: 1980, 140). However crudely, this probably sums up the anxieties of many current practitioners. Buried within this view is the extraordinary paradox that pupils should study and analyse media culture but are to be banned from 'interfering' with it because of their hopeless inadequacies; equally teachers are warned to stay firmly in their didactic seats.

These anxieties are best conceptualized as a fear of inappropriate 'imitation' by pupils on three levels. First, the outcomes of trying to copy professionally produced media texts, especially using the moving image, will be hopelessly poor in quality and will literally fail to be even mere imitations. Second, the act of imitation is a kind of collusion with dominant media forms and with society's invisible models of social and cultural control; pupils are being made to reproduce, not reflect. Finally, the disappointing outcome leads to an even greater mystification of the media, awesomely and invisibly powerful as pupils are left to ponder that all they have learned is their inadequacy. This adds up to a significant issue and certainly one that teachers need to think about.

However, its significance to Masterman and to other media educators was partly a recognition of the inadequacies of much equipment in the 1970s but more fundamentally its source was simply the wish to establish a 'new' subject. In formal education this almost inevitably means that acceptance will only come if the subject can 'prove' its academic worth and be assessed in conventionally academic ways (see Goodson 1993) on the history of school subjects). As considered above, even well-established subjects with strong practical elements get lower status than their academic superiors and assessing the practical (see below) is highly controversial. To some extent therefore, teachers should feel that these 'early' misgivings have been addressed and that media and specifically moving image practical work have accrued some validity through trial and error and through a gradual acceptance into the formal curriculum (see Chapter 1).

Buckingham *et al.* (1995) respond to what still is a very real issue by identifying a number of much more positive 'versions' of production developed chiefly, although not entirely, since Masterman's condemnation. The first, 'self-expression', is the one discussed above (principally in relation to writing), which does have a long tradition within English, although one with a very low current profile. 'Practical work as a method of learning' is another version and certainly has a defined place in many subjects, put more simply as 'learning by doing'. Buckingham rightly argues that there is nothing specific to media work in this approach. However, in acquiring skills and competencies in order to make a moving image text there is absolutely no doubt that a great deal can be learned through the process, to some extent regardless of the product, if the expectations of the pupils are appropriate. Some of Masterman's critique disappears if the users of video cameras actually know what they are doing. This leads to the 'vocational training' version. This version exists principally within the context of specialist courses, chosen by students, typically post 16 and literally related to job acquisition within 'the industry'. The remodelling of the curriculum may well lead to more opportunities for such approaches within mainstream schooling but they are of minor relevance to English. What they best illustrate is that training sessions for pupils may well be very valuable, leading them forward to more critical and reflective work. Such sessions might not have to be led by the English teacher if technical advice is available: this is not an argument for teachers avoiding the acquisition of such skills themselves; it is simply a recognition of the limited training of teachers currently, and a recognition that this need not be a barrier to engaging pupils in the work itself.

The final version of practical production offered by Buckingham *et al.* (1995) is the mode of 'deconstruction'. Perhaps somewhat ironically, Masterman did advocate this version of practical work although he limited it to 'exercises'. For example, pupils might first analyse the conventions of television and then 'try them out' through a simulation (much as suggested in Chapter 4 of this book). Through this process they would demonstrate their understanding of these conventions and also potentially subvert them by deliberately parodying or 'debunking' them. Essentially, this is imitation but with a purpose that goes far beyond imitation. However, as stated, Masterman defined these as very non-technical activities. There are still many reasons why such approaches remain productive and developmental although they are even more powerful if planned as work towards more sophisticated and actual production. This version is also closest to the concept of critical reading, and specifically to the Cultural Analysis model of English (see Chapter 1). Although both of these are conceptualized as modes of analysing existing texts, they also attempt to empower the cultural analyst to do something; in the English classroom such doing might be a range of activities from the exercises sketched above and in Chapter 4 to the production of a complete moving image text that is at least partially an attempt to demonstrate and subvert how moving image conventions 'work'.

For most teachers embarking on a form of practical work, all the 'versions' may play a part. Equally, in a department committed to teaching about the moving image, it may be possible to identify practical projects, spread through the curriculum, that not only build pupils' practical capacities and so address the vocational version at least to some extent, but also allow them to undertake several productions so that they can see that 'self-expression' is possible, as is 'deconstruction'.

So far there has been no mention of equipment. Given the variability of equipment in schools it seems important to offer a range of exemplars that illustrate what can be done with very little, say one old (i.e. non-digital) video camera to many up-to-date cameras and editing suite and studio type facilities. It is also worth stressing that plenty of active learning can take place that really emphasizes the practical production of media texts with no 'equipment' at all. This is no 'cop-out'; the pre-production stage of many media texts is intensely practical and pupils can learn a great deal from engaging with it. It also needs to be stressed here that the moving image can always be 'paused' or 'stilled' and that this is a fundamental part of its construction. There is no paradox, then, in using a still or digital camera as part of practical work about the moving image. Even a cardboard square frame to 'look through' is a significant shift towards being practical in visualizing the realization of a moving image text.

Evaluation and assessment, motivation and ability

Perhaps the final 'issue' for teachers of English when considering undertaking practical work is, put very simply, what to do with 'it' when it finally happens. If, as suggested above, any practical project is likely to have several intertwined elements, then will all, or just some of them, be assessed? Will the teacher or the pupils evaluate the process, the product or both? Can it be justifiable to undertake a moving image project principally because it frequently has a very motivating effect on the majority of pupils and perhaps especially on normally unmotivated pupils? Typically, moving image texts are collaborative ventures; who gets the class Oscar? Has, for example, the pupil 'director' demonstrated high ability or will the teacher's 'A' go to the scriptwriter because in English it is writing that always counts in the end?

This section can only be a brief exploration of this highly complex and very fascinating area of culture. The term 'culture' is appropriate, compared to say art, because pupils are, typically at least, engaging in producing a text with a broad cultural resonance (for example, a simulated news broadcast) rather than an attempt at 'high art' (such as an arthouse film); however, there are plenty of conflicting views about the validity of such a distinction. Given the theoretical complexity surrounding this field, readers are referred to more detailed discussions (Sefton-Green and Sinker: 2000) and this section is designed to alert teachers to some of the more concrete challenges in responding to practical work and to providing a brief rationale as to why they are worth undertaking and overcoming. The rationale is partly inflected by a consideration of motivation and the recognition (considered and developed in Chapter 7) of the growing significance of both 'after' and 'out of' school activities in this arena.

It was not a glib comment to suggest that the scriptwriter might get the 'A'; pupils actually learn a great deal by writing a real script and attempting to realize it in images. They may, for the first time, acknowledge the art of scriptwriting, as normally most viewers (perhaps especially young ones) have only the faintest awareness of a writer's existence in relation to moving image texts. More pragmatically and professionally, English teachers have very real expertise in assessing and responding to writing. It would therefore be a perfectly valid task in English, with a clear learning outcome to assess, to ask any pupil to write a script, and this is currently a regular aspect of practice. However, the task leads us on to the main issue. A script is not a short story in which the reader is expected (and expects) to 'realize' the story in 'their heads'; a script's quality and effectiveness are comprehended in the act of realization, almost always by other people.

To assess a script for its correct English, its use of script-writing conventions and general linguistic coherence is to do a very limited job; in the time allowed for teachers to undertake assessment (especially in English) such limitations are as much to do with external demands as with teacher or pupil motivation. However, this latter point usefully illustrates the need to design evaluative strategies and assessment opportunities that may go beyond current narrow requirements (a National Curriculum writing level for example) and to engage pupils in a mode of work and learning where some conventional assessment approaches are simply inappropriate; the learning itself, however, remains highly valuable.

As in the previous section, the work in Media Education and Media Studies of the past 20 years has much more to offer here than work in an often stifling English curriculum whose narrow and prescriptive confines are controlled by a frequently mechanistic assessment regime. Buckingham *et al.* (1995) has a number of helpful points to make but honestly recognizes that many of the case studies the authors researched were especially weak when it came to both assessment and evaluation and, most importantly, in their conclusions to a lack of genuine and meaningful reflection by the pupils involved. On the positive side, in the English section of an Ofsted review of good practice in secondary subjects, a great deal is made of how the best departments incorporate pupil self-assessment.

In order to engage pupils in appropriate and genuine evaluation, teachers need to organize the practical project into pre-production, production and post-production and to mark each stage by a reflective pause. Divided in this way, evaluation becomes both more manageable and more genuine. The pre-stage might involve learning about the textual form to be attempted, e.g. documentary, trying out the use of the camera and any other technical equipment, some research into the subject and a 'draft' of the text including visualizations like a story board. The emphasis of evaluation here will be on what has been learned and how this knowledge will be used. It might include some reflection on the quality of contribution by individuals and groups. Methods may include the reflective log, probably the prime tool in media studies work of this kind, in which individuals record key events and learning moments in note/diary form; teachers may well provide a set of prompts to focus pupils on what to note and a model of a 'good' example. A version of the log might be tape-recorded as individual comments or group discussions. The latter, i.e. discussion, should form a part of the evaluation process whether recorded or not. If the class has been working in distinct groups then this reflective period is an excellent opportunity to bring the whole class together to pool their learning before they embark on production itself.

Any production period is likely to be both intense and, curiously, potentially slack; this is typical in most schools because there is not enough prime equipment to allow simultaneous use. Given that this is by far the most common scenario, teachers will have to plan for the practical work to go in parallel with other work. They will also have to be very clear about time limits and this helps to put the right pressure on the pre-production work; pupils have to be very ready to undertake their project. The teacher also has to ensure that the criteria (see below) for the project enable pupils to be realistic in their planning and not to be over-ambitious. This realism relates equally to the vital contribution of the post-production period, because pupils might shoot 30 minutes of material but their brief will say 'a 3–5 minute documentary'.

During the production period pupils, however much encouraged, may not be explicitly reflective as they engage very intensely with the task. However, with moving image work in particular, reflection is most certainly happening all the time as the attempt to realize their visualization is tested and as they make rapid adjustments through the practical experience being developed. Teachers can help enormously at this point by observing some of the production work, prompting and helping where this is appropriate, but equally by noting the creative process 'at work' in order to prompt pupil reflection later on. Inevitably, pupils wish to go straight on to whatever the post-production stage may be but it is vital that a reflective period ensues, for example to discuss their experiences and to write an extended entry in their log. As well as having value for their learning and retrospection this reflective pause also focuses on the task ahead, a period that is often far more laborious and even frustrating than any of the work so far.

Post-production, typically editing in some form or another, is a kind of evaluation, given that the group (or individual) is almost always making a selection and refining the text, for example adding music or sound effects, so there must be an evaluative process going on. Once more, this needs capturing, especially before any 'showing' to an audience whose evaluation may be problematic in many ways. One of the key factors at this stage is to engage pupils in a review of all their previous reflections and plans so that reflection upon this earlier material plays a part in their more summative evaluation of their work to date. This attempt at some conclusive evaluation has two other key benefits. First, it provides a basis for the overview evaluation that may well be the teacher's key document for assessment (see below). Second, it helps pupils to gain some perspective on their production and gives them space to acknowledge but also learn from its limitations and its 'faults', helping them to see the importance of process, not just the product.

If the product is to be viewed by an 'audience', then that audience can be a part of the evaluation. All teachers familiar with such moments in Drama work will know that clear criteria and 'rules' need to apply to make this period productive. If all pupils have undertaken evaluation in the format recommended above, prior to the showing, then both audience and 'presenters' have already been appropriately critical of their own work and are sensitized to the difficulties of the production process. However, teachers know they will have a vital role in orchestrating such a session so that criticism is constructive and so that pupils benefit from the session and can make use of it in their final evaluation. For most teachers it is likely to be the evaluation, in whatever final form it is produced, that forms the basis for any formal assessment. This is normal practice in Media Studies but also remains highly problematic as the writing is essentially a secondary medium of interpretation rather than the 'thing itself'. If possible, teachers need to give the moving image texts themselves both the recognition and the status of being assessed.

This is not as difficult as it first appears. Two analogies with writing may help to clarify this. In writing we expect pupils to pay attention to correctness, particularly at the editing stage, but most teachers also value pupils' expression and so positively encourage pupils to 'have a go' at challenging textual forms. Correctness seems less obvious in the moving image but it is just as evident and important in its place. In an interview on television, for example, we see both participants – the subject, and the interviewer. There is no absolute visual necessity for this, but in a 'correct' interview we will have either some reaction shots as the interviewer responds to interviewee comments, or nodding head comments where we simply see the interviewer silently 'nodding' at intervals. In professional scenarios these are filmed afterwards and dropped in by the editor at specific moments, often to mask an editing in the tape. It is extremely valuable if teachers, having already helped pupils to analyse these techniques, then build them into the brief for their production and therefore into the assessment criteria along the lines of 'Your text must include the following . . .'. Such specificity also enables pupils to make much more informed comments when they are in audience mode.

Earlier in the chapter, we considered how some media educators are highly critical of 'mere imitation', especially if it seems to trap pupils into reproducing some of the repressive norms of society. However, the correctness described above is really convention, as indeed is all correctness in writing. Pupils can only really challenge conventions when they develop some genuine understanding of their purpose as well as their simple existence. Practical work is an excellent means for them to develop a much more dynamic understanding of how moving image conventions work. It also helps teachers enormously in having precise aspects of the text to look at and to provide feedback to their pupils. It can lead to providing pupils with a means to subvert or challenge mere correctness. For example, if a camera dwells on an interviewee's face for a long time with no reaction shot, pupils would be able to articulate in their presentation/evaluation that this was not amateurism but a deliberately unconventional move.

Such a move is a form of 'expression' but so is the conscious use of convention. At this stage in the development of moving image education it seems particularly unreasonable to ask pupils to demonstrate a great degree of 'expression', least of all that much-prized notion of originality. There are many creative touches to be made through playing with convention and employing parody; these are very real signs of understanding and interpretation. The potential of ICT is beginning to provide much more genuine opportunities for authentic expression and creativity, but this is beyond the scope of most English departments at present.

In assessing the moving image text as a whole, English teachers need to offer pupils a realistic set of criteria and that is why some specific details such as the use of normal conventions helps to keep pupils focused and to provide achievable goals. A teacher may also feel it appropriate to provide quite prescriptive aims about the 'meaning' of the text. For example, 'the text clearly establishes its main intention': this might be to inform or to persuade or to entertain. Another main aim might be 'the text provides its audience with clear signs of its form': this might be followed by a list of the conventions and other features that pupils should include. As mentioned above, pupils are unlikely to make arthouse films any more than they are likely to write what might be called experimental fiction. Teachers have a very clear role in helping pupils work with textual forms and within genres that they can make some genuine use of. Pupils might well look at the horror genre and demonstrate through their practical work that they understand 'how it works' but their text might be an additional 'scene' for an existing television or film text.

A final point in this complex area is that other imponderable, motivation. It has long been a kind of standing joke in Media Studies circles that the first thing pupils must be disabused of when they have chosen the subject is that they are going to sit about and watch videos, or that they will be making lots of their own. The implication here is not only that pupils are unrealistic in their expectations but that both activities are ones they would very much like to do. Media work of various kinds does seem to be motivating. Equally, working on computers appears to be highly motivating (see for example the *ImpaCT 2 report* (DfES: 2002)) but research has not yet untangled the 'wow factor', that combination of novelty and perceived glamour that generates genuine pupil excitement. Teachers are rightly suspicious about whether much real learning goes on in such situations.

Much discussion above has focused on helping pupils (and teachers) to have realistic expectations when embarking on practical moving image work and on ensuring that there are clear and manageable outcomes. Even so, such work cannot avoid some of the 'wow' factor; indeed, that factor, when properly channelled by the teacher, is extremely powerful and might just be a reason for attempting it. Pupils will put enormous amounts of effort and time into a moving image project; this can be true of other media work but the moving image certainly can be the most motivating. This is very helpful to the teacher in a general way but also with the specific issue of time. Practical projects, especially if they involve filming and editing, will never fit neatly into the little packets of time prescribed by lessons. This factor can daunt even experienced teachers, especially when the curriculum is so crowded. However, pupils are usually very ready to give a great deal of their own time and to work outside the timetable, much as they are for a Drama production. This is a vital element when planning a practical project and for putting pupils under realistic and useful pressure because if they want more camera or editing time then, very often, it has to come from their 'own' time.

It may be the case that the 'wow' factor will gradually fade in the future but it is certainly here for a number of years to come. It may also be true to suggest that there is only a little of the novelty factor within the 'wow' because for most pupils making moving image texts is intrinsically valuable and meaningful in a multimedia and multi-modal world. There is abundant evidence from a range of projects, most notably the 2002 publication *Being Seen, Being Heard: Young People and Moving Image Production* (Harvey *et al.*: 2002), that young people of all kinds are highly motivated when engaged in moving image production and achieve excellent results. A great deal of such activity happens outside formal education and produces texts not easily accommodated within the current constrictions of the school curriculum and assessment model. For some, this may be evidence in itself that once such activities become 'schooled' they lose their attraction for young people, especially those for whom school is often a problematic context. This may indeed be a factor for a minority of pupils but it is not an argument for excluding the majority of pupils from the excitement and challenge of practical moving image work. If English teachers can accept the challenge themselves then the benefits of such work can be firmly established over time.

Documentary

This section focuses on a fairly detailed examination of a practical moving image project resulting in pupils developing a documentary. However, a good deal of the discussion, especially about pupil organization, is equally relevant to the production of a number of other moving image texts and will not therefore be repeated later on. Chapter 4 included some brief illustrations of how limited aspects of practical work could inform pupils' study of documentary and could accelerate their understanding of its construction. One example was of a camera being used 'fly on the wall' style in a classroom while pupils attempt to be 'normal' and of watching the results to appreciate that documentaries have to 'construct' reality as much as fiction does. This approach was extended by suggesting the use of the now extensive sets of training videos which feature 'normal' classrooms and which might be studied (with the pupils as experts) by assessing their authenticity and realism. The other key point observed about pupils making a documentary was that it could be on a subject of importance to the producers and the intended audience. Developing an understanding of the documentary genre leads very genuinely to making an example, and to a final reflection on both analysis and production. As with all moving image texts produced by pupils, it can be very helpful at the outset to make clear that the practical component is at least as much about developing a more sophisticated understanding as it is about the actual product. The emphasis on evaluation and reflective pauses is vital.

Thinking about documentary as a practical project can be broken down into manageable phases. Having studied the form, pupils are aware that its prime purpose is to offer evidence to viewers about an important issue and that much of its interest lies in maintaining the audience's interest through a number of devices. The inclusion of a number of documentary conventions can form a valuable part of the 'brief' and also enable evaluation by pupils and assessment (where relevant) by the teacher. So, this initial stage connects the previous analysis to the beginning notion of a pupil-made documentary for a local audience.

The second phase concerns the identification of a subject or subjects. There are two issues to address at the outset of this subject phase. The first involves a decision about the size of the documentary team. It is quite feasible to make a whole class project work, one benefit being that there is one collaborative text for the class to put their energies into and to evaluate in conclusion. This may still mean the subdivision into teams which are responsible for aspects of the documentary. With a professional production these would be established specialists such as researchers, presenters, technical people (sound, light, etc.) and so on. For most teachers, however, as the learning outcome for all pupils concerns understanding documentary, a different approach is likely to work best. Without expecting every pupil to take every role, the following are desirable activities for all pupils: researching, planning, being behind and in front of the camera, selecting and editing. If the teacher is expecting pupils to use an evaluation log, these roles may be identified as part of the assessment criteria for each individual. With a whole class project, groups can then be given sequential sections of the documentary to produce that can finally be edited into a 'smooth' text. Another approach is to give each group a sub-theme within the overall brief and the final editing can then be done, drawing on that material to create a sequence. The latter approach inevitably means fewer pupils working on the final edited product, a factor that may well be helpful in pragmatic and even artistic terms.

The most obvious alternative approach is to make each team responsible for a complete text. Each team might be focusing on the same subject, so setting up some potential for comparative evaluations and for learning about alternative approaches. Equally, teams might have a broader framework such as 'Aspects of school life' or 'A local community issue' which still allows for useful comparisons but gives a bit more flexibility to each team and provides more variety for the pupils as audience.

Whether a whole class or small group project, every documentary needs a well-defined subject and the teacher may be best placed to determine the subject, partly as a means of ensuring feasibility and of setting realistic expectations. However, there is much to be said for some healthy debate and discussion about what might be an important subject and how it might be defined and presented. Such a discussion might well lead to the production of an appropriate text. Nevertheless, the teacher will have to take what is essentially the producer's role and constantly ask questions that focus the class on realistic aspirations. It may be very helpful if the teacher acts 'in role' as a producer, adopting a very hard-nosed approach so that pupils are challenged more by a knowledgeable, and rather cynical, 'character' than by their more sympathetic and supportive teacher.

Ultimately, a key question will relate to the potential for a real audience. If there is no intention of aiming at a genuine audience then to some extent the class is 'freed' from this constraint. However, for most classes a constraint is in fact a helpful element in focusing their work and a 'real' audience is a valuable part of the process.

As documentaries present problematic issues, the subject will need to define and 'offer' something to an audience for whom there is a genuine concern. The most immediate audiences will be within the community of the school, for example a particular year group, an interest group (sport, leisure interests, environment), even the whole school and its teachers; with more ambitious projects, parents and local families may be included. If the topic is more community-based, another audience may be identified. Even with older pupils, teachers have to work within health and safety constraints and so yet another element in the producer role will almost certainly be to limit locations.

Information videos

The information video is a particularly apt text for a practical project for two key reasons. First, such videos can combine a real subject with a real audience very easily, and second, they are often produced on a low budget with a very limited purpose. A simple example illustrates this point. Some form of 'Introduction to the school' provides an excellent and very real purpose with an intended audience such as prospective pupils and their parents. The class will have their own experiences of joining the school to draw on and, with the teacher's help, will recognize that such videos are typically promotional. This challenges them (in every sense) to select a set of images that promote their school and its environment in the best possible light. Pupils will benefit from looking at and analysing some examples from the genre and from considering related material such as school and travel brochures; some television programmes of the magazine kind also provide useful models of this form of presentation.

This kind of work is extremely effective for helping pupils appreciate the use of shots to create effects and the whole concept of *mise-en-scène* because they very rapidly realize that filming is all about exactly what is in the frame and also about what is very carefully left out or discreetly disguised. As with documentary, it also helps them see how 'natural' behaviour in front of a camera is carefully managed and constructed, especially when close up. A few long shots of the playing fields and the school buildings are fine but once pupils and teachers come into actual focus the 'film crew' soon encounter many problems that help them to reflect on their need to 'create' real scenes rather than just film them. As such professional productions are normally low-budget, pupils can work with more realizable ambitions and with a potential audience which is more likely to admire their genuine skill than suffer from their own inflated expectations.

Such texts, once finished, actually have a local value and even a 'life' and may well be used by the school in its promotional work. It is worth reflecting on the fact that this works at two levels. One is the immediate level of school promotion and the valuable point that such a text can be used many times with different audiences and is reliably providing a consistent message. The second is that such a text is also evidence of the quality of pupils' work and of the school's capacity to develop skills that matter in the multimedia world.

Simulation

It is perfectly possible for pupils to learn a great deal about practical moving image work through attempting to simulate a variety of texts from normal broadcasting. There was some discussion of this approach above, but without including the element of filming. The key factor is for pupils to demonstrate their understanding of a genre or programme category and the practical element enables them to test and consolidate their knowledge. With simulation, another useful factor is that there need not be an attempt to create an entire text but only a significant element within it; two scenes from a soap opera will be quite enough to demonstrate a wide range of characteristics and typical 'devices'. This concentration is also very helpful in aiding pupils in steady improvement of very specific aspects of practical work, the equivalent of drafting in writing and working towards a highly successful final draft. An enormous amount can be learnt from producing two minutes of a news broadcast rather than attempting 20. Simulation also creates opportunities for parody and subversion that can be enjoyed by pupil 'makers' and their audiences, not least because pupils discover that it is much harder to do well than they envisaged and requires just as much skill and effort as the target of the parody.

Simulation may also be very helpful for relatively inexperienced teachers as it can be highly controlled in the best sense. Filming can take place in a single location such as the Drama studio or the school hall and much of the pre-production work can be undertaken in the normal classroom. Pupils can then watch and review their own work and that of the other groups and then revise their simulation before a second filming. This acts as a kind of editing without involving any technical complications.

The story of the making of . . .

It has been discussed above how television is always developing new forms and categories of programmes, often creating hybrids, and that documentary has now many formats including docudramas and docusoaps. Another element, and one that certainly includes film, is the kind of documentary that attempts to capture how a text was 'made'. The advent of DVD in particular allows a film to be released with masses of additional footage of the film but also with some commentary on how the movie was made, including filming of the filming. Such material provides excellent material for moving image education (see Chapter 7).

This 'behind the scenes' approach has its own long history but its more recent prevalence offers a stimulus to pupils to make an appropriate moving image text. For example, most schools annually put on plays, musicals and other performance-related productions. They send pupils on trips, sometimes quite exotic and even adventurous trips. If some pupils can create a moving image record of the production or trip then it offers rich material for an edited version that tries to capture the drama of the process and build-up and then of the event itself, concluding with the reflections of the participants. Such a text will certainly have a very real audience that is keen to see the result. However, this leads to a further point about making a well-crafted text, not just a somewhat indulgent and haphazard record.

From the teacher's point of view, for most of the time she is barely involved. The filming of the process, possibly over many weeks, will normally be done by a few key pupils and so this places particular emphasis on the planning and editing stages. Pupils will benefit enormously from guidance at the outset and from some explicit input from the teacher, drawing on professional examples, of what makes such texts interesting to any audience, not just the participants. Such guidance also helps pupils capture the kind of footage that is worth editing rather than endless hours of tape with no coherence and little potential. Pupils may also need to decide how to make the 'story' interesting by concentrating on some key actors rather than cramming in every participant. In this way all pupils can be involved in planning the project and in editing the results while no time is 'lost' in the filming, all of which takes place outside the normal classroom.

An animated future?

The final section of this chapter reflects on some recent and current work that offers great promise for moving image work in the future; some of these ideas will be developed in Chapter 7.

The rapid development of technology is creating one very significant opportunity for moving image work. In essence, the key development is the increasing availability of software that enables the digitization of images and also digital editing at low cost. Pupils with access to digital cameras can bypass the digitizing stage. The enormous advantage to pupils and teachers is that digital editing can allow the editor(s) to treat all the raw material as always available. With 'drag and drop' software pupils can 'grab' the moving image sequence they want and 'drop it' into the position in the text they are creating; if dissatisfied they can drop it somewhere else or remove it altogether. This technique can apply to existing digitized texts such as films and television programmes as well as footage created by pupils themselves. This makes it both an analytical and a creative tool. Digital editing has so many advantages for moving image work that it is in the genuinely rare category of the potentially revolutionary. The long-term potential will be discussed in Chapter 7.

One example is worth drawing on briefly here to encourage teachers to recognize the potential for their work. It concerns animation. The making of a 'cartoon' was completely beyond the scope of 'amateurs' because of the extraordinarily labour-intensive nature of its production. This was unfortunate in one sense because of the simple fact that younger pupils very much enjoy cartoons of all kinds and have an enthusiasm for the kind of artistic creativity that animation requires. Digital editing means that pupils can create characters/figures for a cartoon and with the advantage of the right software can relatively easily 'animate' it into a short cartoon. Cartoons have the practical advantage of bringing together children's own 'real' drawings and the range of image resources from computers and the internet. They also allow for a much more experimental approach, as the figures created are not meant to look 'real' in the narrowly literal sense. Their figurative nature means that children can make use of the existing 'types' from the world of animation but can manipulate them and combine them in myriad ways. This technology is developing very fast and clearly offers particular opportunities for younger pupils to engage with the moving image in a genuinely fundamental way. For an excellent example see the detailed account of primary children exploring the story of Red Riding Hood in Burn and Parker (2001).

The other sense in which the future can be considered animated is in the certain knowledge that moving image practical work can be the entitlement of every pupil. This chapter has argued that English teachers are far more 'practical' then they tend to think and that they therefore already have plenty of expertise to draw on. Equally, an appeal is made to teachers to consider how valuable such work is to pupils in their overall development and to strive to overcome the narrow prescriptions of the imposed curriculum. The chapter has also acknowledged that moving image work can seem off-puttingly 'technical'. The examples above demonstrate that this need not be the case and that very limited equipment and 'know-how' can lead to very valuable practical projects and good 'outcomes' in every sense. Finally, a few schools are beginning to take advantage of the enormous potential of the digital in all its forms and soon many more will be able to engage in moving image practical work in a far more sustained and exciting way than in the past.

Chapter 6

New technologies and the moving audience

A case has been made throughout the book for moving image education to become central to English teaching. In relation to curriculum developments at the end of the twentieth century, this is (somewhat ironically, given the dominance of the media in that century) still a radical proposal. This chapter is even more radical but based absolutely on the realities of current cultural and technological developments. To some extent the chief areas covered so far throughout the book might reasonably be called 'traditional' areas of media education and even, to an extent, of the school subject English. They clearly have a history in secondary schooling, they have advocates, some teachers are skilled in the associated pedagogy, and they have some recognizable place in the formal curriculum. However, despite this genuine position, they remain insecure and there is still much to do to make them routine elements of secondary English.

While acknowledging this need to stabilize moving image education, there is an equal need to conceptualize this move as essentially 'catching up'. The culture we inhabit is already there and curricular prescriptions are like a dam waiting to burst. So, this chapter explores what might be called the potentialities of moving image work and covers areas which currently have a far less accepted place in schooling. It also offers many continuities with the last chapter as so many recent technological developments invite production as well as consumption; in other words, many young people are involved in technology in an everyday practical way.

Looking for the multi-pedagogue

The prefix 'multi' is becoming omnipresent: multimedia, multi-literacies, multi-modal, multicultural are particularly relevant examples. It is worth exploring whether this is just an example of linguistic laziness, or perhaps techno-slang (like 'mega'), or some profound recognition that our understanding has changed. Certainly many theorists in the field of education are of the latter persuasion. Their work, which will be briefly summarized, is almost exclusively without empirical evidence although it has begun to enable empirical research that is capturing supporting evidence from the field. In England, the initiative known as EPPI (Evidence-based Policy and Practice) has begun a series of reviews of educational research to distinguish findings that have an empirical base and/or offer robust theoretical models that therefore offer scope for use in practice. The English review has focused on ICT and its impact on literacy (Andrews: 2003) but in subsequent work, still under development, there has been an attempt to review the field in relation to moving image literacy in English (Burn: 2003). The findings of this review act as a basis for much of this chapter.

It is also important to help teachers to put all of this into some meaningful perspective and to enable reflection on where changes to curriculum content or teaching approach are worth considering. As an initial stimulus to this chapter, it is helpful to articulate some questions that are affecting English (and other) teachers that might then be answered, although more emphatic answers can only come from teachers themselves if they accept the basic premise and bring into their classrooms some of the questions as ways of helping their pupils explore new meanings.

These questions might first be formulated around specific technological developments that frequently involve images and increasingly moving images. How should schools relate to the internet? Is the school's role a combination of simplistic use, for example 'it is good for research', and of paternalistic protection, i.e. much of the internet must be excluded from pupils? Or should schooling try to engage with the internet in a much more challenging way and demand that pupils develop forms of cyber expertise? Should computer games be viewed as essentially irrelevant to schooling and not even discussed as a phenomenon – basically ignored? Or do they have a place as learning devices, or as texts for analysis and critique? Perhaps more fundamentally, do schools have an educative role in the multi-modal lifestyles of their pupils and, if so, what kind of intervention or facilitation should it be? Chapter 1 has attempted to establish some basic points about what might be termed the 'visual turn'. That turn is the recognition that education for centuries has been dominated by written language and by print in particular, but that for a number of decades the image, in multifarious forms, has been in the ascendant. For many this is a restoring of a balance lost when print literacy became the hegemonic mode. The particular attention by the educational systems of many countries to maintain that hegemony is seen by some commentators (see Cope and Kalantzis (2000), and Chapter 6 for a discussion of the conservative role of the school) as remarkably clear evidence of its imminent demise. The established and the powerful are trying to hold on to their positions of privilege and influence. However, it is also reasonable to say that the death of print literacy has been very much exaggerated; it might be far more productive to consider cultural assimilations rather than replacements.

This balancing act is usefully articulated in making *Moving Images in the Classroom* (BFI: 2000). But it is also important to recognize that the BFI's focus is often on 'cine-literacy' to the very deliberate exclusion of broader categories of literacy and even media education. It is also striking that in defining its four competencies within cine-literacy BFI (1999, 31) includes, as well as analytical competence, contextual knowledge and production competence, the competence of 'canonical knowledge', i.e. the idea that a number of great films should be identified and included in the school curriculum. One contributor goes so far as to suggest that 'the really cineliterate individual is one that really knows how to recognise a great work of cinema and to discover why it is great', and another that 'the ability to list ten major films and film makers from around the world' is a key skill (BFI: 1999, 31). The chief point here is that 'film' has a 'respectable' pedigree in the academy and so can be brought alongside print literacy as a worthy form. This pontificating serves to remind us that what many young people actively enjoy will, almost by default, be unworthy.

This is where the terms 'multi-modal' and 'multi-literate' come in and are helpful to teachers in conceptualizing a way forward. Film has been with us for enough time for it to have many traditions and conventions, schools of criticism and internal debates: all the hallmarks of the academy. It is no longer a new or innovative technology; its innovations are stabilized within over a hundred years of change. Phenomena such as computer games and the internet attract wildly divided and confusing social comment. Should teachers who are already prepared to incorporate moving image teaching of the more traditional kind into their classrooms go further into the much less settled world that young people inhabit?

The multi-literacy movement (although this an oversimplification, it has many internal fractures) would adamantly argue that teachers should embrace the multi-modal world of what Andrew Burn calls 'digi-teens' (Burn and Reed: 1999). There will be a more detailed discussion of this term in Chapter 7. It is worth stressing that this 'movement' has several sources. One source stems from advocates of an essentially constructivist approach to learning such as Bruner (1990), who conceptualize learners as strongly agentive and active in meaning-making. In this view, notions of literacy as a single competence or even as a set of skills are simply inadequate. Vygotsky's theories have had a huge influence on media and literacy educators towards a social model of learning that cannot be narrowed to a teacherly transmission model. They (see for example Lee and Smagorinsky (2000)) argue for the notion of intellectual tools, i.e. ways of interpreting the world that have been developed through both formal and informal learning. Language and its associated literacy is one tool, but the visual language of images and codes is another and both involve the other.

This notion of the complement of literacies is evidenced in the way certain advocate groups have tended to add 'literacy' to another word, e.g. 'computer'. This can be a useful notion, suggesting a repertoire of overlapping literacies. It may also suggest that the acquisition of any literacy, conceptualized as an interpretive system, leads to the capacity to develop many others; in the past we may have been so dominated by print literacy that we could not see 'past' its monolithic status. Other educational theories such as multiple intelligences have also challenged the hegemony of the linguistic.

One of the most coherent theoretical positions has been developed by the New London Group, whose work is especially relevant to English teachers. Their coherence is not to be confused with simplicity, however, and this summary tends to oversimplify: readers are directed to a text such as *Multiliteracies* (Cope and Kalantzis: 2000). These authors' main point essentially is that there is an 'increasing complexity and interrelationship of different modes of meaning' (Cope and Kalantzis: 2000, 25). Their key term is 'design' and they argue that we can identify design, so far, in six major areas: the linguistic, the visual, the audio, the gestural, the spatial and the multi-modal. The last of these 'is of a different order to the others as it represents the patterns of interconnection among the other modes' (Cope and Kalantzis: 2000, 25). In discussing linguistic design in more detail they develop the argument by offering an extended interpretation of design itself: 'the design notion, emphasises the productive and innovative potential of language as a meaning making system. This is an action-oriented and generative description of language as a means of representation . . . such an orientation to society and text will be an essential requirement of the economies and societies of the present and the future. It will also be essential for the production of particular kinds of democratic and participatory subjectivity' (Cope and Kalantzis: 2000, 26). For anyone interested in moving image education it will become immediately apparent that the medium contains all five design elements and the overarching 'multi-modal'. All very grand and all-encompassing, some teachers might remark, but what about the current stuff of English teaching?

Within the New London Group, the work of Gunther Kress is a participating but at times distinctive voice, and frequently the one most directly concerned with subject English. In *Writing the Future: English and the Making of a Culture of Innovation*, Kress (1995) argues for English teachers to acknowledge the visual turn. He reflects on the dominance of 'the technology of literacy – lettered representation' (Kress: 1995, 22) as a force that replaced the previous dominance of orality and that now only permits us to think in certain ways. This intellectual system is about to change fundamentally, because:

Electronic technologies are having effects on the potentials of communication which are as yet incalculable, but seem already at least as far-reaching in their potential effects as the shift from orality to literacy, of the newer shift from literacy to 'visuality'. Their deep effects are noticeable in several domains: in unmaking and remaking social relations; in their potential effects on the basis of the rule-system of language; in their unmaking and remaking of ideas of reading and writing; of authorship and readership; and, perhaps, in the end, though not as yet fully recognised, on the place of language in the landscape of communication, in the semiotic landscape overall.

(Kress: 1995, 22)

Having argued for this fundamental shift, Kress develops a theory of text that is especially valuable for English teachers working in a multi-modal textual environment. He categorizes texts as 'culturally salient', 'aesthetically valued [and valuable]' and 'mundane' (Kress: 1995, 34). The aesthetically valued is the one still most closely associated with English and might now include some 'classic' films as well as literary texts. However, he points out that such texts typically belong to one cultural group in a society, 'Hence what is treated as most valued in a society is a reflection of histories of power within one cultural group, and histories of power and domination between cultural groups' (Kress: 1995, 35). This conceptualization is extremely valuable in helping English teachers think about moving image adaptations in particular and why certain texts get regularly remade.

However, it is the other two categories that are most helpful in the context of this chapter. The culturally salient text is considered against the criteria of significance, within both its own social domain and potentially others; this can include the aesthetic text but its inclusion would be for a quite different rationale. The curriculum would thus include a collection of texts from as many cultural groups as the multicultural society itself contained, something subject in itself to constant changes. The internet might be conceptualized partly as a collection of salient texts, i.e. texts that 'matter' to a vastly diverse set of producers and consumers. Of course, it will also contain many texts from Kress's third category, the mundane, which he considers 'are overlooked, yet they are the texts which are most telling, in many ways, in our everyday and working lives. They form the bedrock of social and economic life. Without an understanding of the mundane text, and without the confident ability to use it for one's purpose in whatever domain, we cannot be fully effective participants in the economic, social and political life of our group' (Kress: 1995, 36). This approach helps English teachers to see the benefits of working with pupils with the texts that inform their daily lives and these certainly include texts from the internet, computer games, mobile phones and so on; only some of these will be predominantly moving image but increasingly they will be multi-modal and the choice of incorporating a moving image will be at the communicator/producer's discretion.

Since the 1995 book Kress has extended his argument in a number of directions (see for example Kress and Van Leeuwen: 2001) and much of his focus has been on the visual, particularly notions of visual grammar. He returns to 'English' directly in one significant article (Kress: 2002) and in a very broad sense in *Literacy in the New Media Age* (Kress: 2003). In the former he argues for a re-invigorated English. He posits three options for English:

> It can become the 'Latin' or the 'Classics' of the present period, and await its demise into irrelevance. It can be dragged into full pragmatic relevance by becoming the subject that deals with 'Communication' both in its own right and right across the school – a new version of 'English across the curriculum' re-branded as 'Literacy across the curriculum'; and equally doomed to failure. Its existence will be relatively assured, as one of the service departments of the school. Its intellectual claims to curricular centrality, however, will have been abandoned . . . The challenge is to develop arguments that pay the most serious attention to the real – new – tasks for English, while neither dismissing the fundamental significance of certain texts nor the real claims of the economic pragmatists . . . Most importantly, for its role as a central part of the new curriculum, it needs to take the present rhetoric about innovation and creativity at its face value and demonstrate how it makes its essential contribution to these.
>
> (Kress: 2002, 18)

For Kress, the key words in English are now creativity, innovation, imagination and design. These terms can become central to English because of the affordances of the new technologies. In *Literacy in the New Media Age* he offers a new theory of literacy; see Chapter Four, 'Literacy and multimodality', where he argues that our previous reliance on linguistic theories to define literacy is now inadequate and that we must combine language-based theory with understandings from semiotics and other visual theories to provide any kind of coherent or relevant meaning to the term 'literacy'. He concludes the chapter:

We are used to imagination of the one kind: receiving ordered structures, the elements of which need to be filled with our meanings. We are already in an era which may be defining imagination more actively, as the making of orders of our design out of elements weakly organised, and sought out by us in relation to our designs. In this, too, there is a relation between representation, communication and the rest of the social cultural world. Imagination in the sense that it was produced by engagement with the written text was a move towards an inner world: imagination in the sense that is required by the demands of design – the imposition of order on the representational world – is a move towards action in the outer world. One was the move towards contemplation, the other is a move towards action.

(Kress: 2003, 59–60)

For most English teachers, the word 'imagination' sums up many of their strongest feelings and allegiances to the subject English. The concept of creativity speaks equally powerfully to them of the role of English in developing pupils' capacities way beyond the functionality of so-called basic literacy (see the opening of Chapter 7). It is the terms 'innovation' and 'design' that are less familiar and even slightly threatening. However, the two negative options for English – stagnation into a dead Classics or the aridity of a communications model – are useful and salutary reminders of why terms such as innovation and design need to be part of a reformulated, future-oriented English. If English teachers accept that they have a very central role in working with pupils on domains such as the internet and in considering cultural artefacts like computer games, then notions of innovation and design immediately make coherent sense. As Kress suggests, we seem to be in an era where terms like imagination and creativity are in the educational and economic ascendant and have a chance to seize the learning agenda to the advantage of pupils and teachers.

The internet

The claims for the transformative agency of the internet are legion: much better to consider initially what we do know about current practices. Much better also to acknowledge that where the internet is arguably transformative is far more evident in the domestic and work settings than in schools. All the more reason to consider how English teachers can make their contribution to pupils' learning and development in the school setting and to plan for an active involvement with children in the future.

It is also important to contextualize the place of the internet in a book about the moving image. At a fairly simple level it is clear that some of the images on, and available from, the internet are in the 'moving' category. It is equally true that much of the material looks relatively static; in some cases it is almost exclusively textual. We still speak of web 'pages', clear evidence of our mental straitjackets. In its shortish existence the internet has rapidly evolved to be an increasingly moving image, moving text and interactive medium. It has also become the most multi-modal medium and the one where consumption and production are most authentically interrelated. There is no need to resort to cyber clichés; the internet is extraordinary and offers us the full range of texts in Kress's terms from the most mundane to the most salient. A consideration of the internet has to feature in any examination of moving image education and has to be conceptualized as both quite distinct from traditional forms such as film and television and also complementary to and evolutionary for those forms (Sefton-Green: 2003). For example it is possible, having entered a website, just to 'watch' the internet: something will almost certainly 'happen' if you do. However, 'browsers' are also the moving audience referred to in the title of this chapter. Internet users seem to adopt a restless stance and to move back and forth between sites as their 'back' and 'forward' buttons allow them to swap around instantaneously. The majority of sites on the internet therefore have some resemblance in mode to television, in that they are increasingly designed to capture browsers and to make them more like viewers and potential consumers.

A final prefatory concern for all teachers must be the problematic nature of the internet as an environment for young people. This problematic nature consists of two intertwined dimensions. The most frustrating dimension is the technical. For many teachers the nature of the school day, divided into short discrete lessons, and the physical location of machines, marooned in over-booked computer suites, makes real use of the internet impossible at times. Many school machines seem appallingly slow to many pupils and their domestic settings frequently offer a much faster and more interactive relationship than school; however, there are a great many children for whom school is the only real setting in which they can access the internet. These interrelated technical issues are one reason why making the internet chiefly a 'research' instrument is a problem in itself (see below). The moral dimension means that schools also have to 'police' pupils' access to the internet and typically limit searches to acceptable sites, often setting up an intranet system that creates a mini-internet; given current technological limitations this is something of a necessary evil but it should be viewed as part of an early phase of school use (see below).

The internet has a role in relation to every school subject and potentially to learners of whatever 'ability' or age. Many schools offer discrete ICT lessons in which pupils learn a range of skills, mostly technical, and so pupils potentially arrive in English able to use those skills, web page design being a good example. However, Ofsted's visits to schools (see Ofsted (2001)), specifically targeted at different subjects' use of ICT, repeatedly find little evidence that subject teachers are aware of what the pupils have been taught. Equally, pupils rarely transfer their knowledge between subjects in school and certainly do not inform their teachers very often about their capabilities. However, the pupils themselves do often bring a range of sophisticated skills, principally from home or other non-school settings. Therefore, an English teacher may need to investigate the ICT skill levels in their class before undertaking any scheme of work that will make extensive use of the internet.

It is important then to focus very specifically on what English teachers can usefully do with their pupils. First, the issue of 'research' on the internet. There is no question that pupils can use the internet for research and can make use of their findings. However, at present, they may simply and blandly be encouraged to 'look at the internet'. This phrase might once have been 'look in the library'. It illustrates the point that one needs to know *how* and *where* to look. English teachers need to be very clear that their pupils do know how to look and for some tasks also exactly where to do so. They may then need to activate this existing knowledge or to teach it directly by modelling research on the internet, possibly in conjunction with a school Librarian. In this way, for example, a lesson might involve research into the moving image, perhaps its history or perhaps the website of a new or forthcoming film. The teacher in this instance will initially be quite directive, first to ensure that pupils are applying their skills and second to create some common understandings. Research building on this might be much more individualized or group-oriented, with pupils making use of the internet's potential for linking concepts and ideas.

However, putting the term 'moving image' into Google produced 2,780,000 hits in 0.17 seconds; 'Hollywood' produced 8,950,000 in 0.05. Research needs a research question and a very clear purpose and a methodology that can be used to achieve the right outcome. There is no contradiction here with the very real pleasure that the internet provides as browsers make what feel like discoveries; the difference is often that the browser has dedicated a large amount of personal and leisure time to having the equivalent of a long ramble through the country. So, having looked at the website of a new film or equivalent, pupils could then 'look for' other comparable sites, possibly even on a 'hunch' basis. They might be looking at the content, i.e. investigating what is said about a film, how it is categorized. Equally, they might look at the implied audience or the kinds of marketing strategies being used. Typically, they could also now look at examples of moving images used within the website, some of which may be from the film's footage, others that are attention devices, part of the site's design. This is just a simple example to illustrate that teachers can make very positive use of the internet for research, especially about the moving image, but they perhaps need to think even more carefully about the nature of the pupils' task because of the tendency for pupils to become mere 'ramblers'.

Research is only one important aspect of the internet in relation to the moving image. Within the broader field of media education, study of the moving image on the internet needs to be part of the critical literacy/multi-literacy project of the New London group and others. Pupils need some explicit teaching about multi-modality, again ideally through teacher, and potentially pupil, demonstration. The web has many metaphorical resonances, one being the browser as 'fly', becoming entangled with dire consequences. More literally, the web needs to be 'read' and 'viewed' as a vast means of representation.

There can be a clear link between pupil research and a critical literacy stance in the simple notion of sources of evidence. Is the source a valid one? Can the evidence, opinions expressed, be backed up by examining other comparable evidence from other independent sources? Such an approach would be standard practice in History. New forms of software can track how a website has been produced, who has sponsored it and what its more hidden links may be; pupils should have the opportunity to make use of such investigative tools. From a moving image perspective, a critical literacy approach involves questioning the images as well as the text. Pupils need to bring in to play the conceptual understandings that they have learned from more traditional moving image lessons about film or television. They are unlikely to do this without a combination of explicit teaching and then further exploration. The development of interactive white boards seems to offer enormous potential for such activities, allowing the teacher to demonstrate and model to the whole class and for pupils then to do the same.

The other element to the argument about the internet's transformative power is that it is not just a resource but a medium in itself. As with the digital editing software discussed in Chapter 5, very rapid software evolution is making contributing to the internet possible for all citizens, and young people are clearly already very active in this process. Moving image material is still more problematic to work with because of the size of the files that tend to be involved. However, even this issue is diminishing as computer memory capacities increase enormously with each 'generation' of machines and as the 'zipping' of files makes them far more portable and gives the receiver so much more discretion about accessing the material.

As has been argued above, the use of still images can be enormously valuable as part of moving image education and English teachers can begin to work with the internet just using still text and still images. However, both moving images and moving text are perfectly possible and will increasingly be so. Another valuable point in this area is that the internet is a domain in which what might be termed the amateur and the professional producer are relatively equal. An enormous amount of internet content is produced by people who are enthusiasts first and web designers second. One outcome is that their sites are less professionally produced but are of very powerful interest to certain like-minded others. This offers a rather different model to pupils compared to undertaking production on, say, video where a number of issues about the 'look' of such material and the problems of mere imitation can arise (see Chapter 5). Many internet sites are clearly 'state of the art' and they are likely to be the ones where moving images are predominant. However, pupils can also first look at and then produce web material that is not imitative but instead essentially focused on doing the best job possible for the purpose in mind.

For example, a number of the practical activities undertaken in Chapter 5 could also be adapted for the web. If pupils have put together a documentary on a topical subject, useful questions for them initially just to discuss would be, 'Should we adapt this for the web, who would it be there for and for how long should it remain available?' Such questions will help focus pupils on considering the internet as a place for their work but not an automatic one. Considering these issues leads to an appropriate reflection on how a pupil-produced moving image text should be adapted for the internet. Should the audience really be conceptualized as any internet user in the world or, much more usefully, should the text be carefully framed and positioned so that it might genuinely attract and be of use to potential consumers, for example pupils from other schools in similar locations?

As mentioned above, the internet exists in a dynamic and mutually influential relationship with other moving image forms such as television and film. Bizarrely, it is even turning radio into a medium that can have images as one can listen to a broadcast while watching the website or listen to the radio on one's cable or digital television. This hybridity is a perfect illustration of the multi-modal interpenetration of almost all media. The place of music on the internet and the extraordinary growth of its significance to young people deserves a book in its own right.

For English teachers, an excellent focus may be websites that literally bring the moving image and the internet together. Film websites have been mentioned above and offer a rich combination of visual resources for film study and for critical literacy, enmeshed as such sites are in a mixture of explicitly commercial advertising, fandom and filmic tradition. Such sites often provide a limited degree of interactivity, especially if aimed at young browsers who expect a game-style format.

The richest source may well be the sites devoted to children's television, as Julian Sefton-Green comments in his study of such sites:

> The spread of the home computer and especially the internet has had a particular impact on children's TV, which is evident from even the most casual of channel hopping today. All the main broadcasters of children's programmes in the UK, from the BBC and Children's ITV to the global multinationals like Nickelodeon, Disney and Cartoon network, maintain extravagant and dynamic websites. Not only are these sites frequently

mentioned by continuity announcers and in adverts, but they figure centrally in design logos and other publicity material.

(Sefton-Green: 2003a, 185)

Such sites are particularly interesting because in one sense they are meant to direct the browser back to being a viewer, but at the same time they are clearly very independent and offer complementary experiences, sometimes even, whether intentionally or not, almost rival activities to the 'mother' station or programme; as Sefton-Green (2003a, 186) puts it 'complements, supplements or substitutes for broadcast programming'. In order to offer these three aspects, the sites must capture and entertain the browser while always referring them back to the 'main' focus, typically a specific programme, but cannot afford to miss this chance to interest the young consumer in other related media products. A key factor in such a hybrid site is its 'interactivity'. Currently a broadcast is still very predominantly a one-way medium; children's programmes that strive to be and 'feel' live, that are almost hyperactive in their involvement of children at every moment and where presenters chat familiarly as if they are in the front room as they speak, are in a sense betraying the medium's lack of interactivity. The use of video-phones, interactive video and viewers sending in emails as they watch are all small moves in more genuine interactivity, but they do not significantly affect the programmes themselves. The study of these programming features themselves would make an interesting project for an English class examining the interface between children's television and websites aimed at children, especially if they could compare broadcasting with webcasting:

The relationship [between TV broadcasting and the web] is part of . . . [what] needs to be considered as the changing nature of '-casting'. Here the prefix stands for 'broad' (as in broad-casting . . .) and 'narrow' or web casting. It also covers the concept of online publishing or indeed any of the changing institutional relationships media producers might have with their audiences as a result of the new interactivity implicit in the online environment. Here, one key question is what role online '-casting' has within the gradual move towards fully integrated broadband interactive communication – which is promised to deliver audio-visual content into the home at the viewer's demand and specification . . . At least according to its

producers, children's TV is at the cutting edge within the broadcast industries, as they develop in concert with the impact of
the web . . . Children here are very much the testing ground
for the future – or, as some cynics might say, are being educated
to behave as the online consumers of the next generation.

(Sefton-Green: 2003a, 186–8)

Sefton-Green's tentative conclusions are that these sites do provide a
modest level of interactivity and offer a form of social relationship
with programme producers and participants. Children do have
more independence in relation to the site as compared to the programme. However, his point about the grooming of future consumers is bound to interest English teachers. From a general media
education perspective these sites offer excellent opportunities for
examining critically the claims that they represent the cutting edge
of broadcasting and webcasting. As regards the moving image,
they provide a precise focus for examining how the two media use
still and moving images in their attempt to create complementarity.
The interactive dimension of such sites and their mirroring of game
environments leads us on very logically to perhaps the most controversial element in the book.

Computer games

Computer games have, in the main, passed through the moral panic
phase and entered the stage where they are mostly assimilated into
various leisure domains. Strictly speaking the games are not just
computer-based, many are only playable on dedicated hardware.
The past few years have seen the enormous growth in the games
console market: the Dreamcast has come and gone (since its acquisition by SEGA), and Microsoft's XBOX and Nintendo's Gamecube
vie for market leadership with the Sony PS2, the second-generation
Playstation. To keep our focus simple the term 'computer games' will
be used. The proliferation of hardware and games themselves helps
to explain why they are now part of the techno-furniture. Rather like
film and television, it is increasingly a particularly controversial text,
rather than the medium itself, which attracts attention. Nevertheless,
teachers and parents maintain a deeply ambivalent stance towards
them. Some of the main anxieties concern the content of many
games which are completely dominated by violence in innumerable
forms; the violence is often linked to all kinds of typically 'macho'

activities, particularly involving vehicles and speed. The games are perceived to have an almost hypnotic, addictive effect, especially on boys. As a result they can be considered very anti-social and physically problematic because players are static and 'hunched over' the screen. Another concern is always the more hypothetical one about what games players might otherwise have been doing instead of playing, such as worthy reading or healthy exercise.

Research in the mid-1990s resulting in the book *Young Children, Videos and Computer games: Issues for Teachers and Parents* (Sanger *et al.*: 1997) was very clear about schools and teachers, as regards computer games:

> In general, schools don't countenance them on the premises . . . The initial response of most teachers . . . was one of disapproval. They believed there was no educational reason to have them on the premises and they had little knowledge of those very popular commercial games which contained strong educational elements . . . Certainly their impact upon children's behaviour has been noticed by teaches in stylized play in the playground and to a far lesser degree in subjects chosen in written work but such effects were not particularly prominent within our own findings.
>
> (Sanger *et al.*: 1997, 2)

In the conclusions of the book they remark:

> Our research tended to confirm the view that children, like other members of society, develop language and forms of physical expression within specific contexts . . . we found very little evidence thus far, that children were being particularly affected by the fictions of computer games or videos . . . the traditional view of children knowingly acting out in response to their screen-based experiences or willingly suspending their disbelief whilst engaged in them, seemed to hold good.
>
> (Sanger *et al.*: 1997, 176)

This ambivalence of teachers (and some parents) stems from this recognition that most games players seem in all other respects entirely normal; they just happen to have a very intensive hobby. They also gain enormous enjoyment from playing, and much playing is actually with a partner and to that extent social. Games players do actually have many like-minded associates and read very technically demanding texts about games, in print and on the internet. And in an age of parental street phobia, games players are usually safely at home and tucked away in their bedrooms having no disruptive effect on the domestic space of others.

More recently, games have been supported as potentially educative, either as enhancing motor skills or as more generally developmental in both cognitive and affective domains. BECTa has sponsored some interlinked projects to investigate some of these more recent claims, the BECTa Computer Games in Education project (2002 and ongoing). All the studies are small-scale and all the findings are tentative, but the emergent view is that a range of games offer differing kinds of potential benefit. The element of the project that trialled games in school found a mixture of effects but positive elements such as increased motivation, higher engagement, positive collaboration and greater opportunities for a focus on citizenship issues.

Rather like the effects debate about media violence, the controversy about games is set to run interminably. No doubt empirical studies, such as by BECTa and by Sanger and his team, will find evidence both for and against their use and their effects. Like the internet, games are very multi-modal experiences for the player(s) but, in contrast, players never 'browse'. Rather like a book for a fully engaged reader, they 'enter the world' of the game. There are a good number of other analogies with books worth considering from the English teacher's perspective. First, they have to be read and comprehended, rules understood and applied. Like reading, much of the skill comes from prediction and anticipation, from testing hypotheses and some trial and error. Many seem to engage players in a kind of fantasy world, something usually highly approved of in literature and film. Many games, at least to an extent, have characters, settings and plots. In fact an interesting question for some games is to treat them as a more literary text and see what narrative dimensions they have and to what extent they matter to the player. Games are not just about winning but about an almost readerly satisfaction with closure. Many are organized in levels and as players progress they get closer and closer to a sense of an ending. Games, also like books, come in versions and series. The key characters move into another challenging arena and the player once more invests in the fantasy world. Old favourites can be returned to as and when one wishes. Rather like avid readers (and literary critics), keen players get together to talk about their favourites, swap 'texts' and recommend new ones. This comparability to books has a particular resonance for English teachers but does not quite do justice to the games themselves, which provide many things that books cannot, not least in their use of the multi-modal. It seems important for teachers to engage with them as a phenomenon and to treat them seriously but not essentially negatively, not least because many games have content that is likely to gain immediate parental/teacher approval. Given the multiplicity of games and game formats, English teachers might adopt the following approach which considers games from a number of perspectives including as a social phenomenon, as multi-modal texts and as psychological 'tools'. There is also some opportunity to engage with production.

As a social phenomenon, teachers might begin by enquiring what pupils know about and do with games. This enquiry will require some sensitivity as games' 'territory' is very much non-school and certain games which have '18 certificates' may well be played without parental knowledge. Equally, games are rather like designer items, signs of something about the individual/group that bears a representational quality, so there may well be difficulty in getting pupils to discuss and reflect on games with any seriousness or authenticity. In mixed classes, in particular, there may be gender-related issues evidenced through boys' possessiveness about games as a territory. There is increasing evidence that gender is much less of a factor than it either actually once was or was presumed to be. The Sanger study found that the female negativity resided not in the players but in the majority of female adults, both teachers and parents. To overcome some of these issues the teacher might initially adopt the social science stance, asking what 'we' know about games, what we know about their appeal and popularity, why some parents are anxious about them and so on, keeping the personal out of the discussion. Some research on the internet about games might be very productive, especially for pupils (and teachers) who have little direct experience of playing themselves.

Any such investigation into computer 'games' will reveal that the term is a very loose one. Some texts are absolutely and only about playing and winning or losing, although they too can be examined as moving image and multi-modal texts for their design and use of representation. But many games have far more elements than the win/lose binary. What they all have in common, like language, is that they are predominantly rule-governed.

Some games really are very like books, particularly of the quest style of narrative. In games like these the player becomes a character and an agent within the world of the game and has to 'move though' its virtual buildings and landscapes. The potential value of these games has been discussed in more detail elsewhere (see for example Zancanella *et al.* (2000)). However, it is worth stressing here that they combine many of the qualities of the book-style narrative with some of the features of a filmic/televisual story. Some are constructed as simulations, with a set of characters perhaps setting off on a journey and crossing a landscape. The reader/player has to make decisions at many levels, from what to take on the journey to how to survive a disaster, always with the 'characters' in mind. Other games in this *oeuvre* are more like fantasy fiction, often set in Tolkienesque universes full of people and creatures of pseudo-mythical origin. Here the reader/player often has to discover the world and its 'rules' through trial and error and often through a combination of literal reading of 'found' texts and precise observation of visual clues. Zancanella *et al.* quote a young man recalling his involvement with games:

> It was so immersive to me, so powerful because I became a part of a different world, a world where my participation, my courage, my dedication were vital, crucial to the world's continued existence. A world where I was being evaluated mostly on how hard I was willing to try and how clever I could be.
>
> (Zancanella *et al.*: 2000, 87)

They treat the narrative-style games as literary texts and, adopting a reader response stance, investigate the games for their textual features. However, they also note throughout the impact of the visualization of the games' world and the richness and brilliance of the graphics, the importance of sound, print and other symbols. In essence they are describing the multi-modality of the narrative. These more text-like games offer rich opportunities for teachers to work with their pupils on analysing both the visual design of the environments and the nature of the stories being 'told'.

More recent research into the latest fantasy-style games (Burn and Schott: 2003) suggests several additional reasons for considering games as forms of salient text. First, such games draw very extensively on both literary and pre-literary material. The form of game playing where the player is at times the main character, *being* that character, but at other times is watching over him and nurturing him in a style resonant of the Olympian gods, provides a textual environment closer, they argue, to classical and traditional oral narratives. The text is best understood as a text-event happening partly in the game and partly in the reader's mind; no two events are ever the same. The hero figures, often called 'Heavy Heroes' because of their physical manifestation and their predictability, for example the way they fight, their use of a favourite weapon and so on, all have some of their origins in figures like Achilles or his equivalent from Japanese narratives or, more often, a hybrid combination. The figures are also modelled on the twentieth-century superheroes of the Superman and Batman types. Such figures have to be 'larger than life' and 'memorable' as the player needs to build up knowledge of how to 'be' in the game world. This 'being' involves understanding how the visualization works and how certain camera movements, 'swooping into battle' for example, are both signs in the game and symbolic resources that the player can manipulate and influence.

For the English teacher there is enormous potential for engaging with this semiotic and multi-modal environment. In a sense the characters are bundles of semiotic attributes drawn from a range of cultures and traditions: simply asking pupils to visualize and try to describe what characters are 'made of' and what they 'do' should lead to a very rich discussion. Equally, asking what they represent and how they are represented offers an excellent means for considering the portrayal of, for example, the hero. The teacher could enrich this by using clips from films and passages of text to help pupils consider the historical tradition behind the games. Using either a whiteboard or projector it will also be possible to look at the games themselves (relying perhaps on pupils to bring in their own examples) on the screen and to analyse camera movement, point of view and so on; all such games have both official and unofficial websites with enormous amounts of additional material to review and draw upon. The focus on computer games also offers opportunities for much 'traditional' work in English in which reading, writing and speaking and listening activities are built around the examination of games: see Catherine Beavis's (2001) account of a secondary school project and Haas-Dyson (1997) in relation to primary pupils.

One of the most interesting family of games is the SIMS. The essential principle in any SIMS environment is that the player actually builds the world and peoples it with characters and arte-facts. Typically the player constantly has to make choices, all of which have consequences. Because SIMS is such a success, and so much more like the kind of game that parents and educators might approve of, it is worth devoting a little space to. The blurb on the back of *The Sims* makes a good starting point:

> **From Will Wright,** the creator of SimCity, comes a new strategy game that really hits close to home! Create an entire neighbour-hood of Sims and then run or ruin their lives.
>
> **Help** them pursue careers, make friends and find romance – or see what happens when you make a complete mess of things! Open-ended game play gives you the freedom to set your own goals and chart your Sims' destiny. It is your neighbourhood and they are your Sims. Whether they prosper or perish is completely up to you.
>
> **Create your Sims,** design their personalities, skills and appearance.
>
> **Build** a neighbourhood of Sims, design and create rooms, choose wallpaper and floor coverings and even landscape the garden.
>
> **Buy** Furnish your home with furniture, electrical appliances, plumbing, lighting and other accessories.
>
> **Live** Control the lives of your Sims as you guide their relation-ship(s) and careers for better or worse. You can even tell their story by creating Sim web pages to share with the world.

Readers may find this language somewhat disturbing. Its blunt emphasis on an almost fascistic control of the 'people' and their environment may seem even appalling. However, it is time to play the cliché 'it is only a game', and that is what children and young people are doing when they 'play'. The SIMS environment is, as it says, a strategy game with open-ended play. No two players will play the game exactly the same and they will be interacting with the resources of the environment in a creative way.

As a multimodal environment SIMS has other interesting features. On the visual side, figures and buildings are 'realish' looking but are also clearly cartoon-like in form; the designers are deliberately avoiding the hyper-realism of more 'shoot 'em up' games. This effect makes the environment look much more like a child's doll's house than a battle zone. The player can continuously revise the visual landscape, move characters around and make them interact. Once 'programmed', characters continue to move and 'act' within the environment. There is sound, principally some sound effects and some music.

In almost every respect, SIMS appears to enact the function of play that all young children engage in once they bring toys into their play, toys being any object that will fit the child's need. Some readers might feel anxious that SIMS and comparable games remove the imaginative element from play. This would be hard to prove either way, but it also seems fundamentally misguided. Children seem to engage with SIMS very intensively and their creativity is constantly in play, principally in a visual mode and in a three-dimensional environment; unlike the doll's house or the toy garage, the structures are always revisable and improvable. The rules mean that players who 'neglect' or make unthinking changes in their world find it develops problems that they then have to solve.

In many ways then, this game and potentially many others may be best conceptualized as pyschological tools. Just as objects in play are tools of the imagination in the young child's world, so the artefacts of a game's environment may be psychologically equivalent. The sophistication and challenge of the game's environment may well help children develop their thinking and creativity. The BECTa studies mentioned above are exploring this potential and the other sources cited above all show, in qualitative ways, how children's engagement with games is both creative in itself and can be utilized by teachers to further that creativity.

To return to games as a phenomenon: they seem set to be a feature of the semiotic landscape for the forseeable future. They have been an enormous commercial success, so much so that the money spent on their development and profits to be gained now frequently outweigh the traditional Hollywood blockbuster movie. As such, they too have huge, expensive marketing campaigns, a wide range of associated products and sometimes make the crossover to a different medium – Lara Croft becoming a film is a spectacular example. Far more games are derivative of successful movies, but as such they help to ensure continued profits and popularity – James Bond and Terminator type games again being good examples. This aspect of the games industry certainly deserves the attention of English teachers. Again it offers rich opportunities to develop general understandings about the media industry but also more specific ones about moving image and visual design.

New games are partly so expensive to develop because their production values are now so high and so sophisticated. This would tend to suggest that children could never engage in production in any meaningful sense. In the current school setting this seems likely to be the status quo. It might be argued that the interactivity of many games and the sense of agency for the player has at least some affinities with being a 'producer'. However, it might equally be argued that this is more a clever psychological effect of the game than any real understanding of how it has been designed.

Little work has been done around games' production. The 'Shared Spaces Project' has made an interesting start (Sefton-Green: 2003a; Willett: 2003). The setting was an informal Saturday school in which a group of youngsters had explicit instruction in professional-level software and, having acquired a reasonable competence, attempted to make their own games. They found the process highly challenging and also frequently frustrating. Nevertheless, they kept going and appeared to derive considerable satisfaction from what they produced; perhaps most strikingly the majority of the group have returned for another year's course, so there will be further evidence of the potential 'effect' of such opportunities on young people.

A number of points arise from this experiment. One of the main aims of the project was to attract and support children from a disadvantaged area; this it did and appears to have every chance of continuing to do so. Schools clearly could evolve informal strands to their work of this kind because it is proving to be highly effective in motivating such young people. They are, in every sense, 'working hard' to learn the skills, engaging in the discipline of a long commitment to a project and developing capabilities of very real use in the world of work. As much of this chapter has argued, they are becoming highly literate and productive in the predominantly visual world in which they will be adults; endless catch-up, print literacy 'progress units' appear to have very little benefit for many disaffected young people; all they do is confirm the disaffection. If the curriculum does become more flexible, then it seems that such projects offer interesting models of how young people can take a productive role in their lives and that school might become a site for such renewed energy. To some readers the technical aspects of game design may seem remote from their expertise and interest. However, this section has endeavoured to encourage English teachers to think of games as an important 'new' genre to add to their teaching repertoire, especially from the perspective of multi-literacy and multi-modality. Kress comments on the irony of the notion that 'standards' are always perceived as in decline in *Literacy in the New Media Age*:

> At times I watch our son and his friends – and it *is* boys usually – playing around with their Playstation. The skills which they demonstrate – skills of visual analysis, of manual dexterity, of strategic and tactical decision-making at meta-levels – leave me entirely perplexed. It is not clear to me that these children are victims of a decline in mental abilities. All the games make use of the visual, but they always make much use of much more: there is a musical score, there is rudimentary dialogue, and there is writing – usually as in comic strips, in a box above the rest of the visually saturated screen. The speed at which the written text comes and goes can be adjusted. The pace at which it is set by the players is always too fast for me to read: I can never follow the text fully. Occasionally, I have attempted to test whether the players have read and followed the written text, and have found each time that they have, I have lagged behind. But in lagging behind in reading, I have not, at the same time, been paying attention to the other features of the screen and of the game, all moving at great speed, nor have I been physically manipulating the controls.
>
> There are an astonishing range of skills and abilities at issue here, which those who make assertions about standards seem not to have taken cognisance of in any way. Clearly, the skills of reading which are at issue here are not the skills of reading which the school still focuses on. However, they strike me as much more aligned with what the young may need later in their lives.
>
> (Kress: 2003, 173–4)

This may seem too anecdotal for some readers but for many parents it is likely to align with their own anecdotal observations of their children. Some readers may also feel that the children of academics are not representative of the range of pupils that they normally encounter. But even with these reasonable caveats there can be no doubt that the reading behaviours observed are so highly skilled that they are of little value in school (as far as we currently know).

Perhaps it is better to say that they are hardly *valued* in school and that in the longer term this is much more worrying. If any of the arguments and predictions of the multi-literacy lobby are even halfway right, then schools absolutely must change.

As argued in Chapter 1, English teachers, in principle, remain student-centred and genuinely interested in the culture of their society, including the recognition of the fact that the young have a sophisticated form of culture of their own and that they have a relationship to the culture that the teachers themselves relate to. The internet and computer games are especially provocative examples of the culture of the young and increasingly 'the culture' more generally. These phenomena are not merely the technical territory of the school ICT teacher; they are much more part of the arena of the English teacher, areas for analysis, reflection and production. It is also vital that they are conceptualized within the field of media in English, and particularly moving image and multi-modal work; conceptualized in such a way that they become part of a dynamic examination of cultural development in which young people feel authentically engaged.

Chapter 7

Imag[in]ing the future

English teachers historically have been much possessed by the concept of 'imagination' and, since the advent of the National Curriculum and the National Literacy Strategy, more concerned about its decreasing presence in their classrooms. And this concern centres, as always, on their desire to make the English classroom a place where the imagination is prized and enjoyed by the pupils themselves. Whatever the inevitable idealizations of the child and the classroom that this suggests, there is no evidence that such aspirations are either insincere or without value.

'Imagination' as a term derives from the Latin *imaginari*, 'to form an image of, represent, fashion'. The word 'image' appears first in Old French, where it means to produce an artificial imitation or representation and is related to the Latin *imitari*, to imitate. What these etymological complexities have in common is the basic notion of the created image, the representation. We make images of the world in the external world and we make images in our heads, some coming from the external world and some coming from our human capacity to create and invent. It would seem likely that we have been using moving images in our minds since some form of consciousness developed and certainly for a much longer period than we have been using spoken language and even more so for writing; we have been producing moving images in the world, as it were, for a tiny part of our history. In that short period, the development of moving image production has been truly extraordinary; it is difficult for us to remember this given how dependent we have become on the presence of the moving image in our daily lives. How much more difficult must it be for children to imagine life without its omnipresence?

These opening remarks are intended partly to remind us that, historically speaking, we have barely begun to explore the place of the moving image in our cultures. They are also intended to make a claim for this development as consistent with the concept of our mental powers to imagine. What might be termed the visual impact of the moving image seems to make it relatively easy to store in the long-term memory, making it into both an affective and cognitive resource. One specific issue for English teachers is its 'memorability', as children frequently remember the film better than the book, or, at least in some instances, struggle to distinguish between their own mental pictures, visualized from a print text and the 'imported' images from a moving image text: one example below will consider how we might exploit this point in the classroom. In a period dominated by nineteenth-century models of assessment and typically memory tests, this is a very frustrating problem for teachers and children alike. It is easy to see that in a classroom freed from at least some of these constraints, it becomes part of the fascination of studying both print and moving image texts; more about this later in the chapter.

This chapter looks ahead, and quite rightly so given the rapid developments of moving image technology, but also because the enjoyment of now 'traditional' moving image forms such as cinema and television is proving remarkably enduring despite the proliferation of new technologies. Persuading English teachers to look ahead with enthusiasm is quite a task given that so much of what they are asked to do appears to require them to look back, particularly in relation to the history of print texts. However, there is a very strong case for a forward-looking stance, even an urgent one, given how remote school activities seem to be becoming from cultural life more generally. The case being presented begins with concepts of the child and debates about what that concept is in a multi-modal cultural environment. It revisits the rationale of English teachers to make connections with notions of the child/pupil and moves on to consider what this offers for our future citizens. A theme throughout this chapter is whether the twenty-first-century child is as 'different' as is often claimed. The evidence, when weighed carefully, suggests that there is a difference, and it principally centres on notions of identity, notions that allow children to be more culturally resourceful in the multimedia age. It argues for a revised version of the Personal Growth Model, positing 'emergent subjectivity' as the new concept. It draws on some recent examples of practice that currently seem to be well beyond the reach of most schools and teachers; however, all of the examples are drawn from the work of English teachers (though some of the context is Media Studies in relation to English). These possibilities are also tantalizingly close and so need to be anticipated. This proximity raises some questions about changes needed in teacher preparation and ongoing training.

Digi-kids and digi-teens; digi-teachers?

This and subsequent sections include many voices, the voices of academics and teachers but also the voices of young people. They are intended to produce something of a chorus that will support English teachers in their fundamental wish to help young people prepare for the future having benefited from a challenging consideration of the past. In many instances the voices refer to actual classroom work and should add further to the store of ideas that teachers can draw on to develop their own teaching, particularly, though not exclusively, of the moving image. This section begins with a consideration of our concept of the child *per se*.

David Buckingham begins his book *After the Death of Childhood: Growing Up in the Age of Electronic Media* (Buckingham: 2002, 3) as follows:

> The claim that childhood has been lost has been one of the most popular laments of the closing years of the twentieth century. It is a lament that has echoed across a whole range of social domains – in the family, in the school, in politics, and perhaps above all in the media. Of course, the figure of the child has always been the focus of adult fears, desires and fantasies. Yet in recent years, debates about childhood have become invested with a growing sense of anxiety and panic. Traditional certainties about the meaning and status of childhood have been steadily eroded and undermined. We no longer seem to know where childhood can be found.

He goes on to comment on how children are represented in what seem profoundly contradictory ways: on the one hand 'increasingly seen as threatened and endangered', and on the other 'perceived as a threat to the rest of us – as violent, anti-social and sexually precocious' (Buckingham: 2002, 3). He reviews the reactions to these perceived changes, which are predominantly of the moral panic type. His analysis of these reactions (Buckingham: 2002, Chapter 2) would make valuable reading for any English teacher, as it would help to clarify for them the pressures they experience from society in the shape of parents, nervous head teachers and intrusive inspectors and also the internal anxieties they feel in their *loco parentis* role. This latter role is intensified for English teachers, who also assume an unusual level of moral guardianship partly formed in the Leavisite tradition of cultural protectionism.

In another useful review of these issues, *Consuming Children: Education, Entertainment, Advertising*, Jane Kenway and Elizabeth Bullen (2001, 1–2) comment on just how anxious teachers in general can feel.

> Teachers . . . are . . . often bothered and frustrated by the children in their care. 'It is *so* hard to be a teacher these days', says one teacher.' 'Kids are so different.' They are often considered more troublesome than students of former decades. They are more easily bored, restless and hard to control. They are also less attentive and respectful, and far less interested in their school work. Many seem to come grudgingly to school. They are apathetic and disengaged when in class, 'turn on' mainly with their peers and seem to get their pleasures, find their identities and, indeed, live the 'important' parts of their lives elsewhere – out of class, out of school. Further, they are seen to subscribe to the sort of materialistic and hedonistic values that schools claim neither to accept nor promote.
> It is often the case that when teachers and parents try to explain the behaviour of 'young people today' they look to 'the media' – in particular, commercial TV, computer games, popular youth culture and advertising directed at the young. Moreover, the media is blamed for kids' short attention spans, is seen to render them passive, to undermine their capacity to play independently, to entertain themselves and also to threaten their creativity. In addition, it is seen to corrupt their morals by favourably disposing them towards violence, individualism, hedonism and materialism . . . In this view the media discloses too much and exposes young people too early to the unpalatable and the forbidden.

It seems reasonable to expect that all teachers, as they grow, older find that kids are becoming different, but we might do well to recognize in that comment that it is at least as much the teachers who are becoming different; they would be very strange if they were not. However, even with this cautionary comment, it is worth acknowledging that the view that 'kids are different' comes from all sides including empirical research. So, in what way are they different in any sense that truly matters and, if so, should English teachers be reflecting on this difference? For example, does the description above from Kenway and Bullen, particularly of the school apathy of children, ring true for many teachers?

The answer to this question about difference can be answered much more positively. The playful term 'digi-teens' has been borrowed from Burn and Reed (1999). The article focuses principally on the work of one group of Year 11 girls who are working on the making of a trailer of the classic Hitchcock film *Psycho*. The girls attend a specialist media college and are working with digital editing equipment that is not yet common in schools, but these contextual advantages are not the key point. The article is illuminated throughout by the girls' written reflections on their work and on transcripts of their conversations about the project on a number of levels. The last section of the article considers the issue of their sense of their identities, particularly in relation to the horror genre and its portrayal of the female.

> These girls bring histories of encounters with popular film that are an important part of their work in Media Studies. Holly and Gwen's account of spending weekends screaming over slasher movies forms an important backdrop to how they have made sense of *Psycho*; indeed, Gwen is now able to explain explicitly how horror movies often play on our society's naive conceptions of childhood and innocence, relating to this the Bulger case; and Holly can make the connections between *Scream* and *Psycho* that appeal to viewers like her: 'There's definitely something intimidating about the young vulnerable woman, because it's part of our culture, that we're more vulnerable than men.' And in suggesting a re-release for a modern audience, the teacher here allows for different social identities of the girls to be brought into play – the part of themselves that is that new audience, its immediate points of reference Wes Craven and Tobe Hooper; and the parts of themselves that can imagine the older audience represented by their parents. The other crucial role is that of the 'media expert' – like pupils

whose sense of self acquires the feeling of what it is to be a scientist or mathematician, they have a sense of special knowledge and skill:

Lorraine: I can't watch now without going, 'Oh that's why they have done it.'
Abby: Exactly, you know why it's raining, and why she's wearing black and you know why he's wearing white and ra, ra, ra.

Students often complain after a few months of studying the media, that they can no longer watch anything on television without an analytical and critical eye, that it no longer becomes 'fun'. However, when you question them further, they are actually very proud and excited at acquiring this 'eye'. Their interview reveals how the act of digital editing has been a powerful emotional experience, one which has changed their sense of self, and provided an excitement that spills out into the street:

Abby: Like, normally staying in school till six would just be your worst nightmare but we actually got really into it last night and like HEH, HEH, HEH [exaggerated triumphant laugh] and we walked out, like, with a smile on our face, as we were so satisfied it had worked!
Holly: We did, we talked about it on the street, 'cos it was so satisfactory.

And this change in their sense of self, of what they can achieve, carries forward for Lorraine into her possible future self:

Lorraine: I mean, after doing this, I was like on the borderland between Film and Media [A level] and now, after doing this I am definitely doing Media, it's so satisfying . . . I'm better at, I was better I think at the written work and now after editing this, and we're not like the most – people who are really amazing at editing, so I thought we did this . . .

This sense of excitement and achievement, which the speed and capacity of digital media undoubtedly helps to produce, has been a common thread in our work on non-linear video-editing, offering a practical and enjoyable experience to disaffected pupils, extremely able pupils and a small group on an alternative vocational programme . . .

(Burn and Reed: 1999, 17–18)

These researchers are also advocates for this kind of work but even with this caveat there can be no mistaking the sense, as they put it, 'of excitement and achievement'. The girls are dealing with a genre, and an especially salient text, on a number of levels. Their 'difference' seems to lie in their self-awareness. They are experienced consumers of the moving image but now they are also exercising very real control over moving image text as a cultural resource for their own creative and critical capacities. As young girls they are aware that they are young girls dealing with representations of the female that may seek to define and limit them; there is some real pleasure in this conceptual understanding, especially as it now allows them to play with it rather than be played with.

And this brings us to another factor in relation to difference which will be addressed during this chapter. Can we really say 'digi-teens'; should it not be either 'digi-boys' or 'digi-girls'? First, the moving image appears to introduce a new dynamic into an old complexity. English as a subject has long been perceived as a feminine domain: put crudely, a girls' subject. Whether this is accurate or not, certain statistics speak for themselves: most secondary teachers of English are female, the majority of university undergraduates in English are female and the achievement of girls (as measured by examinations) in English is significantly higher than that of boys. The recognition of this phenomenon has generated an almost media-style moral panic about boys' underachievement in English, especially in literacy. However, the picture in Media Studies is considerably different. It is popular with both genders and attracts a broad range of abilities, and this trend continues at university. So little is known about the Media teaching workforce that no figures are available to make a judgement about how gender is reflected. If anything, work with the media is sometimes argued for because boys become more motivated just by it becoming their focus. Is moving image work in particular somehow a way forward through the gender impasse?

This section began with the voices of girls because we see them discovering their ability to 'be technical': still, it might be argued, very much associated with the masculine. Part of their excitement and sense of achievement stems from their evident surprise (and delight) at their own success. So clearly, moving image work can motivate girls. The work itself is, however, extremely and *positively* gendered in that the girls, as a group of girls, are reflecting on portrayals of vulnerable females. From their discussion it seems that they find this reflection empowering. The theme of gender will be explored further through this chapter and some conclusions offered later on. The next extract principally features boys reflecting on identity in an equally sophisticated way but begins with some girls' comments to show the way media work generally provides a reflective tool.

In an article by Kevin Lemin (2001), a piece of action research, he develops a critique of his own practice and of the role of practical work in his classroom where Media Studies and English are integrated as GCSE courses. What made him question some of his assumptions about the purpose and value of such work stemmed from the written and spoken comments of the pupils and from some of the materials they produced. These were not moving image texts but in essence they might have been, and the key point is much more about their sense of themselves than the nature of a particular medium. As he concludes the article he first comments on some work by girls:

> In their magazines, Natalie and Claire showed an excellent implicit understanding of appropriate style, language and layout. I asked them to explain and justify their choices:
>
> *Claire:* Modern styles . . . we just try to use, like, what we use, 'cos we know then that other people will understand it . . . less like reading a newspaper and more like reading about your kind of people . . . it stops, like, your sitting down and reading it!
>
> *Natalie:* A lot of teenagers relate to language like that rather than the formal language . . . you wouldn't find teenagers talking like that to teachers . . . if you're in a group or just reading a magazine you can relate to it a lot more.

Both students were showing an understanding of one of the key connections between language and audience: that a major function of genre-specific language is to create a feeling of inclusion, and that a crucial aspect of this *inclusion* is the *exclusion* of others. Natalie formalised her understanding of this in her Supporting Account:

> In a teen magazine the language is completely different to the language used in a political newspaper or found in a book. The language is relaxed with a lot of slang. The language of a magazine can help the teen of today relax from the stresses and strains of life. It also helps to create a sense of identity and belonging.
>
> (Lemin: 2001, 40)

Lemin develops this point further when reflecting on his initial discomfort with the very deliberate macho style of some of the boys.

Paradoxically, I repeatedly found myself asking students to explain and justify to me something that was intended to exclude people like me. In the boys' groups this was especially pronounced. One group of boys chose to do a sexist *FHM*-style men's magazine. In interview I began by questioning their understanding of the term 'stereotyping':

Clive: It's putting certain people in a group and then portraying them in a certain way.

Kevin: It's not true.

Clive: (with heavy irony) Any geezers who don't like the mag are like sad geeks and stuff. It's like people who don't read this mag are sad and boring and don't have a life.

Me: Have you gone along with these stereotypes?

Clive: Yeah!

Kevin: (triumphantly) YYUPP!

Clive: That's why I buy *FHM*. 'Cos it's ideal. It's funny . . . and lots of pictures of women as well. But it's very funny.

Me: So in your Supporting Account, would you write this? . . . that you've gone with the jokey tone of these mags, because that's something you enjoy?

Clive: Have done . . . tried to be satirical.

This was the one of the brightest groups in the class. They are clever students who understand satire. They know that stereotypes are 'not true' and they know that this kind of magazine is 'loaded' with stereotypes, yet they were happy to adopt it as a model. Throughout their work, there was a knowing and ironic tone showing an understanding of media manipulation of audience, but they were not interested in giving their work over to parody and critique because they are *part of that audience*. Instead, they seemed to be seeking to relate to the genre on three different levels simultaneously.

First, as teenage boys forging personal and group gender identities, they found in these magazines a crude but potent tool (the casual objectification of women is not an unusual feature in the social interaction of male teenagers). Second, as intelligent human beings it was important for them to be seen as partially distancing themselves from the magazines – using them as a source of fun and adopting a satirical stance towards them. Third, they saw their media production as a rare opportunity to work outside what they perceived as the rather earnest 'politically correct' agenda of the normal school curriculum.

This three-way interplay between irony, identification and a desire to offend liberal sensibilities is exemplified in one particular article they devised: a questionnaire entitled 'Are you a bloke . . . or a joke?' To each question there is one 'right' answer proving that 'You are normal' and 'a geezer' and two 'wrong' answers – one indicating that the reader has gone too far in his manliness and is displaying excessively aggressive, even murderous tendencies, and the other indicating that:

> You have picked up the wrong magazine. This is not *Woman's Weekly*. This belongs to your son. Give it back to him and go back to watching *Animal Hospital*.

The correct answers all revel in stereotypically 'laddish' behaviour (excessive drinking, fast cars, promiscuity, infidelity) in a way that shows amused awareness of the stereotypes *and* identification with them.

The degree of identification is evident in these extracts from their personality profiles:

. . . the common bloke . . . enjoys going down to the pub with his mates and finds bird watching great fun (nudge, nudge) . . .

a sporty man who enjoys having a laugh . . . enjoys looking at women and sees them as objects of desire, almost in a sexist way.

. . . isn't scared to say what he thinks . . . a ringleader . . . couldn't care less what's going on in the world, about politics or anything else that's serious . . .

. . . doesn't care where money goes and could easily blow a fortune on useless junk.

Basically our magazine is aimed at the average Jack-the-lad.

Precisely what I would like students to criticise in a men's magazine – that 'one-of-the-lads' tone of conspiratorial misogyny – is exactly what they like about it. In fact, an interesting side effect of this work was that students began identifying with the task to such an extent that they became more 'laddish' themselves.

(Lemin: 2001, 41–2)

As with girls working on *Psycho*, these boys enjoy their complicity with laddish texts while working against the grain of them and showing up their macho extremes and absurdities. Again, what seems to be different about these future citizens is that they can enjoy the crude humour generated by a certain form of male identity but they are not controlled by it; indeed they show some sophisti-cated control of it. So, boys can be highly motivated by media work and there seems little doubt that moving image work would be even more motivating. It can be tentatively stated then at this stage, that moving image work both stimulates and motivates both genders but without patronizing either; differences in gender can be a part of the interest of the work, not part of the problem.

While the teachers and their lesson content may be atypical of much 'normal' practice, these are, in other ways, just ordinary pupils in regular classrooms and they are working within the frame-work of conventional qualifications, within the school setting. The teachers are learning a great deal about these 'different' kids, how they are different and what potential this offers for 'excitement and achievement'. In a review of this issue, Hurrel *et al.* (2001, 176) list the following epithets that have appeared in the past ten years: the computer generation, screenagers, cyber-denizens, net generation, N-Geners, young navigators, Nintendo Generation, D-generation, techno generation, electronic generation, cyberkids, netizens, cyber-flaneurs and Generation I; they do not claim that the list is exhaustive. What this plethora seems to suggest is a search to find the right term because of deep adult unease about being able to categorize, and in that sense control, these 'aliens'; it is clearly linked to the kinds of concerns that Buckingham reviews above about the alleged death of childhood.

However, the digi-difference offers many positive attributes. The level of both self-consciousness and self-awareness evident in the talk of both boys and girls above does seem to be a very important part of what makes the 'digi-teens' at least relatively different. This may well have some of the negative traits associated with being also an image-conscious and designer label generation; heightened awareness can produce intensified anxiety; neuroses such as anorexia clearly do have a very real link to mediated images of the female body. The digital image in this sense becomes an image vulnerable to cynical manipulation and distortion. It might be argued that giving pupils the chance to understand how to manipulate an image, perhaps of themselves, whether moving or not, provides them with a healthy insight into the power of such control. The case for acknowledging this kind of 'difference' leads to final consideration of the dominance of the Personal Growth Model (see Chapter 1) of English in teachers' thinking and practice.

Teaching differently?

The question of differences has become a main problem that we must now address as educators. And although numerous theories and practices have been developed as possible responses, at the moment there seems to be particular anxiety about how to proceed. What is appropriate education for women; for indigenous peoples; for immigrants who do not speak the national language; for speakers of non-standard dialects? What is appropriate for all in the context of the ever more critical factors of local diversity and global connectedness? As educators attempt to address the context of cultural and linguistic diversity through literacy pedagogy, we hear shrill claims and counter-claims about political correctness, the canon of great literature, grammar and back-to-basics.

(Cope and Kalantzis: 2000, 10)

This world of differences is certainly the world of the moving image, the world where the 'visual turn' has happened and is understood as part of a fundamental set of shifts, already much discussed in this book. At this point the emphasis is different and asks teachers to look much further ahead than current schooling seems to permit. In the much quoted *Multi-literacies* book there is an impassioned chapter by James Gee, following on from the quotation above, about addressing difference as a potential set of inequalities. It is a remarkably wide-ranging yet densely argued chapter (Gee: 2000, 43–69). Its focus might somewhat reductively be summarized as a theory of identity formation in the era of fast capitalism: in other words, what kind of digi-citizens may emerge in the multi-modal world?

Gee examines what appears to be a remarkable convergence between fast-capitalist discourse and educational theories, especially of learning.

Networks and networking, within what I call distributed systems, are the master theme of our new 'new times'. This theme is redefining what we mean by intelligence, as well as changing the shape of business and schools and by setting up a new logic for a new capitalism. In fact, new business and new schools – fit for our 'new capitalism' – are progressively aligning themselves with each other and converging on such notions as 'communities of practice'. In this new world, social class works to create characteristic 'kinds of people' in characteristic 'worlds'; people and worlds differentially 'fit' for the new capitalism by their orientations in and to that world. The result is the emergence of one new kind of person on the historical stage: the 'portfolio person'.

(Gee: 2000, 43)

For Gee, this 'portfolio person' has many very positive characteristics and the imagined school she might go to will be a much more interesting and challenging place than those that typically exist now.

In a section called 'Kinds of I's', he examines in detail two 'real' female students who are considering their potential life worlds: put simply, one, Emily, from a typically advantaged home; the other, Sandra, disadvantaged. Both have a highly complex and rich sense of what identity is, but quite different concepts of their life trajectories; Emily's self-concept is of high achievement in a range of dimensions, Sandra's is of a reactive life in a chaotic life world. What makes the analysis so powerful is that both girls provide highly detailed and profoundly revealing self-portraits that ultimately suggest, Gee argues, that Emily is a 'new capitalist portfolio person in the making' whereas Sandra may face a struggle to survive 'mired in the backwaters of the old capitalism' (Gee: 2000, 61).

English teachers will recognize here the differences that pupils bring to school normally marked in linguistic registers. So, 'what is so new here?' seems a fair question. Gee is clear that portfolio people can do well in the fast-capitalist world but they are likely to be quietly assimilated; others will be utterly marginalized and the potential for eroding negative differences will once more be lost. School retains one potentially unique element in what it can offer and that lies in its development of new forms of critique that can help both Emily and Sandra. School needs to accept that pupils are different and that they are growing up differently. English teachers need to work with this, not against it, and this will require some reconceptualization of their philosophy of the subject.

The issue is with the Personal Growth Model (see Chapter 1), and it is twofold. First, it may allow for too much emphasis on the 'individual child' in the sense that there is an individual and somehow organic identity at stake. This is not an argument for simplistically treating children as emergent 'portfolio people' but instead for a perspective that both celebrates and challenges the 'Kinds of I's' that society formulates. Where do pupils encounter the kinds of I's that they might be? Essentially in the media, principally in moving image media, defined in the broad sense used in this book. For example, what kind of 'I' can you be in a computer game (see Chapter 6)? In this sense it may be much more valuable to consider 'subjectivity' as the key term rather than the 'individual child'. We all have a subjective view of the world formed from many sources, and equally we are subjects within that world. One sign of emotional and intellectual maturity is the realization of this fundamental aspect of consciousness. English can then both celebrate and develop subjectivity while through its critical elements it helps to develop in pupils that key awareness of what subjectivity 'means'. Second, in its definition in 1989 at least, it focuses on the 'role of literature in developing children's imaginative and aesthetic lives'. No theory of identity formation or view of childhood could possibly now be based on a notion that literature is the primary means of pupils developing as imaginative and aesthetic beings. There is no paradox at all in positing that the experience of literature may well provide a unique element in such development and that this alone justifies its continued place in English teaching. But if English is serious about engaging with pupils' imaginative and aesthetic lives, then it must put the moving image in the centre of the subject.

Perhaps English teachers might have little conceptual opposition to this proposal but they might baulk at the epithet 'digi-teachers'. It is one thing to adjust a pedagogical stance, but perhaps a very different one to embrace the digital age so comprehensively. Most of this book has sought to stay within the bounds of the current capabilities of teachers and schools, but in this chapter it is the future that is examined: not some vague far-off vision; on the contrary, it extrapolates from currently developing practice.

If first we take a new 'model' of English, 'emergent subjectivity', defined as *a view of the individual as a site of contesting and emergent identities which seek to comprehend the world through the consumption and production of cultural resources*; then second we consider the child, like the pupils above, far more as agents in the world, actively seeking and challenging notions of identity including what childhood is, as a result we have a much more positive and powerful position as teachers. Perhaps the first step is a recognition that there is no going back: as Buckingham (2002, 207) puts it:

> We cannot return children to the secret garden of childhood, or find the magic key that will keep them forever locked within its walls. Children are escaping into the wider adult world – a world of dangers and opportunities, in which the electronic media are playing an ever more important role. The age in which we could hope to protect children from that world is passing. We must have the courage to prepare them to deal with it, to understand it, and to become active participants in their own right.

And, as he argues, this puts schools and teachers at the centre of what is important:

> Education is very much the key to the whole process. Educational institutions, broadly conceived, can play a vital role in equalizing children's access, both to media technologies and to the kinds of cultural capital that are needed to use them most productively. They can provide the means and the necessary support for participation in the media, of both the kinds identified above. And they can develop children's ability to protect themselves from – or, more positively, to understand and to deal effectively with – the broader media environment.
>
> (Buckingham: 2002, 205)

For education to achieve this goal it, and media education within it, will also need to change:

> Historically, media education has largely been characterized by forms of defensiveness: it has been motivated by the desire to protect children from what are seen to be the moral, cultural or political shortcomings of the media. In recent years, however, this approach has come to be questioned, not least as a result of research on children's learning, and on classroom practice. There is a great deal more that needs to be known here, particularly about the ways in which students progress in their learning, and how their understandings of the media might transfer to other areas of the curriculum. Nevertheless, we do now possess a rigorous and coherent model of media education, which has been highly influential internationally. From this contemporary perspective, media education is not confined to analysing the media – much less to some rationalistic notion of 'critical viewing skills'. On the contrary, it seeks to encourage young people's critical participation as cultural producers in their own right.
>
> (Buckingham: 2002, 205–6)

This emphasis on young people engaging in production and critique is exactly what James Gee is arguing for above. Young people are already different, but that difference may just be exploited rather than valued. What is at stake here is the notion of citizenship, and education still holds a primary role, as Buckingham elaborates:

Like many of its advocates, I would see media education as a
very significant site in defining future possibilities for citizenship:
If, as Rob Gilbert suggests, the struggle for citizenship is partly a
struggle over the 'means and substance of cultural expression' –
and particularly over those which are made available by the
electronic media – it is essential that the curriculum should
equip young people to become actively involved in the media
culture that surrounds them. Apart from its broader social and
cultural benefits, such a curriculum would encourage children
to have high expectations of the media themselves.
As I have indicated, some critics have argued that such developments are emerging in any case. The new digital media are
seen by some of their advocates as bringing about precisely
the kind of active, participatory citizenship that I have called
for here. Jon Katz, for example, argues that the internet provides
children with opportunities to escape from adult control, and to
create their own autonomous cultures and communities. My
own analysis has been somewhat more sceptical, both of the
evidence for such claims and of the technological determinism
on which they are often based. Certainly, the new forms of
cultural expression envisaged by enthusiasts for digital media
will not simply arise of their own accord, or as a guaranteed
consequence of technological change: we will need to devise
imaginative forms of cultural policy that will foster and support
them, and ensure that their benefits are not confined to a narrow
elite.

(Buckingham: 2000, 206)

His term throughout is 'media education', a subject that currently
exists only within English. It is the teachers of English who have
both this opportunity and this responsibility to find the way forward.

In that sense, English teachers need to accept the 'digi-teacher'
epithet. In the long term there are some issues about technical
knowledge that teachers will need, but in the short term the 'digi-
teens' seem very happy to work with teachers and to share their
sense of 'excitement and achievement' with them. Mathieson's
epithet of the English teachers of the 1970s, the Preachers of Culture
(Mathieson: 1975) reminds us that culture has long been at the
centre of English teaching but that the stance of English teachers
has already evolved beyond the idea of 'saving' the elite few: perhaps
the more realistic term 'teachers of culture' can now apply?

Teaching creativity and resourcefulness

In moving towards the final words of the book, the question arises as to what the English curriculum will look like as it returns to its authentically progressive mode, as the intolerant prescriptions of the 1990s steadily diminish. The pressures of the capital 'L' Literacy movement are producing some powerful reactions (Goodwyn: 2002a) and teachers are reflecting on what they consider is the essence of English. One key word, discussed above to some extent, is the 'imaginative'; perhaps the other most frequently cited is that difficult term 'creativity'. Some particularly significant classroom work supported by the BFI offers an exciting way forward and a glimpse of the future curriculum. The definition of creativity offered by Burn *et al.* (2001) makes an excellent starting point:

> *Creativity* is a word much in evidence in policy circles at the moment (cf. NACCCE, 1999). We use it cautiously, as it raises as many questions as it answers. We feel it is worth employing, however, as many of the observations we made about the students' work at the first seminar were to do with, broadly, the aesthetic nature of the moving-image texts: the sense of students developing stylistic signatures; exploring the aesthetics of different film and TV genres; using the moving image as a way of registering, maybe even transforming, their sense of self; and working, in their new texts, with a set of cultural references from their own experience. The word 'creativity' has a difficult relation with media education, whose rationale is largely derived from traditions of sociology and textual criticism: it is not mentioned, for instance, in Media Studies syllabuses. Similarly, it does not appear in the sections of the English National Curriculum in relation to the study of the moving image (though neither does it appear elsewhere in the Order, demonstrating that English has similar problems with notions of creativity). Burn (2000) argues that the idea of creativity in relation to moving-image production work is a valuable counterbalance to more functional approaches to media education, but that we need a model of creativity that moves away from vague post-Romantic conceptions of self-expression and artistic genius. Rather, we need to describe how creativity might be a loose label to cover the processes by which people represent and thereby transform aspects of their world and themselves

through the representational resources the culture makes available.

(Burn *et al*.: 2001, 36)

This deliberately broad conceptualization fits extremely well with the idea of 'emergent subjectivities' as a model of English. It is also principally focused on the moving image as the chief cultural resource for many young people. Before exploring the importance of the above project in more depth it is worth examining another classroom example because it illustrates this creative process working within the capital 'L' Literacy and quietly challenging it.

Collette Higgins (2002) reports on her action research project, the main aim of which was to help reluctant boy writers improve; this is one of the imperatives of the Literacy movement and part of the moral panic about boys and English. However, the project itself took a bold and brave decision to use film. Higgins comments:

> After interviewing some of these writers, I was interested to find from our discussions that boys often draw ideas for stories from television, video and computer games as well as from reading. Boys who rarely read outside school said they mostly used ideas and themes from these media for narrative composition.
>
> (Higgins: 2001, 27)

As a result she decided to test whether studying the narrative technique of short film could help a group of Year 6 boys to improve their writing by developing a better understanding of how to incorporate visual detail into their typically action-driven stories:

> From a close analysis of the pupils' writing, it is evident that using a film text can and does bring an added dimension to writing lessons. The writing becomes more 'three-dimensional' once pupils realise they have control of the reader's eye and senses, and can direct the reader's attention in a variety of interesting and effective ways. This was achieved by drawing on pupils' interest in film and action but slowing the action down through the use of camera techniques in order to provide enhanced detail.
>
> It is useful to compare and contrast those aspects that directors and authors use to draw in the viewer and reader – suitable texts were identified for extended work with this class for the

following week. We also discussed criteria for choosing texts that appeal to all learners but with added dimensions for 'boy appeal'. The importance of choosing high quality, multi-layered texts cannot be underestimated. In the analysis of the stories from the more competent writers, including the 'reader' in the target group, these were found to be of a higher quality because the pupils were able to draw on a range of literary knowledge, gained from reading, in their writing. From this evidence, the use of film texts may well be more important in supporting reading than writing, as more interest and enthusiasm for reading will result in better writing.

(Higgins: 2002, 35–6)

She continues by addressing the situation as faced by primary teachers working within the Literacy Hour paradigm:

It is entirely possible to teach NLS word, sentence and text level objectives through the use of film text. The project incorporated the construction of sentences in different ways to support inference and imagery. This work was undertaken in the first part of the lesson with appropriate links made in shared writing when the pupils had some experience to draw on. All pupils, including less able writers, felt able to 'have a go' at using these particular constructions in 'supported composition' and in independent writing. Pupils were further supported in using these forms 'at the point of writing' through the guided sessions. They provided examples and reflected on their success in using the language forms during the plenary sessions. Clearly, in the short term, pupils were able to transfer these techniques into their writing. These techniques would need constantly referring to and building on, though, to ensure that they became embedded in the long term.

(Higgins: 2002, 36)

So moving image work can very much aid creativity even within the mechanistic and frequently functionalist mode of the Literacy Hour. However, it is the glimpse of the future that is especially powerful:

The balance of different approaches – video viewing, whole class discussion, 'time out', collaborative and independent working – maintained a good pace and variety for the different learners.

The pupil tracking records of the more reluctant writers show a high level of interest and engagement with the visual text through comments such as 'engrossed' and 'listened intently'. Some difficulties (not knowing what to do) were noted at transition points, indicating that the teacher needs to ensure that pupils are quite clear about the next task at these points in the lesson. Also, frequent reminders about the writing stage (and its features) the children were at, helped boys, in particular, to focus on particular aspects at appropriate times. For example, taking away the worry of accurate spelling and handwriting at the drafting stage helped pupils to focus their attention on compositional aspects. It is worthy of note that some pupils who did not contribute to whole class or guided discussion were, nevertheless, able to transfer the techniques discussed into their independent writing.

And as for pupil enjoyment? The material certainly captivated their interest and motivation. They sustained a high level of engagement through several viewings of the film and developed a keen interest in the main character. I am sure their questions about *El Caminante* – 'Who is he?', 'Where did he come from?', 'Where did he go?' – will provide them with rich material for a future sequel where these young writers can further explore the use of camera angle, colour and sound to improve their narrative writing skills.

(Higgins: 2002, 36–7)

These findings are important because they show the potential to begin the revolution from within the castle walls and, especially because these pupils are at primary school, the potential for them to develop as producers of both written and media narratives seems really exciting. If they could arrive at secondary school already excited by the potential of moving image texts and seeing them as part of the cultural resources available to them for all their English work then they would be very resourceful pupils to work with.

The final example for consideration provides the most enticing view of the future. It relates to three projects undertaken under the auspices of the BFI, all aimed at providing children with the latest software so that they could make media texts and edit them with all the advantages that digital editing can offer (Burn *et al*.: 2001). The work was appropriately experimental and the results offer some real insights but also some challenges for our future development. The key to the research is the framework under consideration by the researchers as a means of conceptualizing what digital editing provides as a creative tool. Their view of *creativity* has been quoted above; the other two chief elements are *literacies and communicative practices* and *social roles and learning styles*. They comment in a way that supports many arguments put forward throughout this book:

The framework was developed from a long list produced by, and discussed by, the group. This was subsequently shaped by the project leaders, who categorised these processes of digital editing under three headings. These headings are provisional and overlapping, but refer to broad categories that frequently arise in the (admittedly scarce) literature in this field.

Literacies and communicative practices refer to approaches both in schools and in research, which imagine work with the moving image as a kind of literacy. In schools, this is often because teachers of media are English teachers by training, with elements of linguistics and language study in their training and experience, rather than the pedagogies and rationales of, say, art teachers. In research in the field, the use of the language analogy is frequently made, often developing traditions in the fields of semiotics, media studies and linguistics that we cannot fully acknowledge in this article. Raney (1999), who examines the case for the idea of 'visual literacy', explores the idea of visual communication as a kind of language, and how this idea has emerged historically. Kress and Van Leeuwen (1996), propose a grammar of the still image, partly basing their theory on traditions of visual semiotics, and partly on those of functional linguistics, in particular the work of M.A.K. Halliday, whose work has a strong influence on the models of language English teachers work. Kress and Van Leeuwen argue particularly strongly that, as the field of communication has widened in recent years and continues to do so, to include increasing quantities of visual material, in the future we will need new languages to describe these forms of communication, and we need to equip pupils with these languages. Burn and Reed (1999) have argued that aspects of digital editing are language-like: the visible strips of video and audio material in editing packages are edited and revised by users in ways that resemble, in some respects, the construction of sequences of language and the processes of redrafting that English teachers encourage students in.

(Burn *et al*.: 2001, 36)

However, they also see some limitations in their thinking:

> In the model on which the studies in this article were based, it becomes clear that the sense in which editing might be a literacy is left too vague, giving the teachers in the project too little on which to hang their account of their students' work.
>
> (Burn *et al*.: 2001, 36)

Their third category again resonates with much of the argument of this book and particularly in relation to the idea of pupil identity:

> The third broad category we have chosen is *social roles and learning styles*. This category reflects the fact that the theories of language, communication and culture we wish to build on, and the practices associated with them, are strongly based in social theories of learning and development. Recent research into media audiences (Buckingham, 1996; Barker and Brooks, 1998) and into forms of digital production (Buckingham *et al.*, 1999; Sinker, 2000; Burn and Reed, 1999) emphasises that young people interpret and construct texts in the contexts of their cultural and social experiences – indeed, that no utterance can be made or received other than socially. So social roles to do with cultural capital – young people as viewers of the moving image on film and TV – and to do with social acts of communication – writing and reading, speaking and listening, making and receiving – will all be important here.
>
> (Burn *et al*.: 2001, 37)

The project is very focused on digital editing and does not claim beyond that focus, but in the context of this book much of their thinking resonates within moving image education in its much broader sense. The somewhat arbitrary appearance of the moving image in the English curriculum looks far more now like a defining moment but one where the impact of that moment has only partially been recognized. But does this 'model' seem to work with the three practical projects undertaken by pupils in years 8, 10 and 13?

Many aspects of the model seem to be tentatively confirmed. In particular, all three of the studies included here emphasise the plastic nature of the digital text, and how the students make good use of this feature to revise, experiment with aesthetic choices, re-order sequences, articulate sound and image. All three note how quickly the use of particular kinds of technical language develops, and one study notes the value of this as a more precise instrument for collaborative work and decision-making. All three evidence the aesthetic work of students: the use of prior cultural knowledge of image, genre and audio-visual codes; the ability to make aesthetic evaluations; the sense of the students' social and cultural selves caught up in the expressive work of the piece they are making.

(Burn *et al*.: 2001, 47)

However, they feel the model is 'too vague' about 'filmic literacy and how it might or might not be like print literacy' (Burn *et al*.: 2001, 47). They also feel that not enough attention is paid to 'how pleasure, rather than fuzzy sentiment glued on to cognitive activity, might be an integral part of it, linked to the aesthetic effects the students are trying to create, and the ways in which their sense of self is tied up in this kind of expressive process' (Burn *et al*.: 2001, 47).

They are rightly tentative; the exploration of digital editing is a genuinely new educational phenomenon and looks set to challenge many of our overly narrow assumptions about the creative capacities of young people. One Year 10 pupil involved in one of the projects commented about his group's work on the film *The Matrix*, 'usually we're told . . . what we're meant to be doing . . . but in the editing suite we've got complete freedom, we're not told at all what we have to do up there, we can do anything' (Burn *et al*.: 2001, 46). That sense of excitement and achievement is present throughout the comments of the pupils in the project.

The model itself was developed directly in relation to digital edit-ing and is presented in the article as a table but is considered here as offering a much more general conceptual framework for an English curriculum in which reading and writing the moving image are normal practices and are seen as fundamentally interrelated and essentially creative processes. To take the statements on creativity first:

Aesthetic understandings and decision-making; 'knowing' when something 'looks good' or 'finished'.

Stylistic signatures; ability to manipulate style, tone, mood.

Identity and cultural knowledge – how it is used, expressed, e.g. understandings of genre and how they are expressed. Level of confidence with which personal identity is explored.

Personal authorship – having themes, ideas, preoccupations that are articulated in the work. Degree of confidence in articulating these.

Having a critical eye.

Differential awareness of different audio-visual codes – do they have strengths in manipulating sound, or images, or in combining them? Awareness of the rhythms of editing, and of energy and movement in the shot.

(Burn *et al.*: 2001, 35)

These statements have enormous potential in a number of ways. They can act as criteria for pupils and teachers to consider existing moving image texts and for evaluating pupils' production work. They also act as a set of guidelines for English teachers to help them think about moving image work, as in does task 'X' provide pupils with opportunities to demonstrate these outcomes? Similarly, the statements about social roles and learning styles, with some minor amendments, offer some clear ideas about designing moving image work that would engage pupils in this range of challenging activity:

Planning – how far ahead, with what level of detail, and how provisionally?

Ordering, filing and naming – how does the student organise his/her material?

Risk-taking – guessing, experimenting, willingness and ability to change their mind; using the 'preview function'.

Role allocation – who takes on technical, social, artistic, organisational roles; ability to subordinate personal agenda to group vision; sharing tasks and input; making space for others.

Use of meta-language – ability to abstract, hypothesise, reflect back upon work.

Admitting what they don't know – willingness to seek help; willingness to help others, mentoring role.

Articulation of preferences.

(Burn *et al.*: 2001, 35)

These statements have a clear relationship to the tradition of media practical work in schools (see Chapter 5) but the very inclusion of one word, 'artistic', changes their nature. The emphasis is strongly on experimentation and the dynamics of the creative tensions between the individual and the group.

Their final element, *Literacies and communicative practices*, is borrowed somewhat playfully here for a different rationale. Let it be considered as a check-list of skills for the English teacher of the future. The question might be: 'How confident are you in making use of the following skills/elements in your teaching?'

Technical skills – use of effects, timelines, adeptness and speed of manipulation.

ICT skills – managing the software (storing, naming, filing, setting up screens).

Arrangement of desktop – awareness of the spatial nature of the medium/screen, changing the scale of the bins and timelines.

Awareness of the plasticity of the medium, how it is endlessly provisional.

Addressing an audience – what the needs of an audience are – balanced against the expressive desires of the student.

Structuring a narrative or presenting a case in video.

Making the medium invisible (e.g. using subtle transitions).

(Burn *et al*.: 2001, 35)

Currently this would daunt many teachers, and rightly so; they have had no opportunity for training and have very few role models to emulate but they would be very creative teachers indeed with these capacities.

Moving swiftly on

Lack of training for teachers remains a major obstacle to moving image education in every respect. The enthusiasm and vision of trainee teachers is very real (Goodwyn and Zancanella: 2003) but they acknowledge how little opportunity they have to use the moving image in the classroom. The prescriptions of initial teacher training are such that very little time can be devoted to media education generally, never mind the moving image specifically. However, there is a growing knowledge base within the profession and the extensive quotations above demonstrate how it is growing at the theoretical and practical levels. Many of the pupils, of course, are 'already there'. There is no point in concluding this book with a vague wish list of training needs; it is better to round off with some simple key points that attempt to summarize the real likelihood for the role of the moving image in English.

Moving image texts will not replace print texts in English but they must displace some of the time devoted to them. As the 'home' of Media Education it is vitally important that attention to the media in English is increased generally. This should begin in the primary school where attention to moving image texts could have substantial educational impact. The minimum in secondary English would be a unit of work per year focusing on moving image texts and developing progressively for pupils a vocabulary and depth of conceptual understanding; such units should always contain an element of practical work. Undertaking practical work will involve a steady increase in the quantity and quality of equipment, partly made possible by technological improvements and partly by steadily diminishing real costs at the same time. The moving image texts may well sometimes be studied in complement to other forms of text but for most of the time they will be treated as salient texts in their own right.

As this change is consolidated in practice so professional understanding and expertise will develop and eventually training opportunities will evolve and initial teacher training likewise; the logic may well be the other way round but this is the effective pattern for 'bottom up' curricular changes driven by teachers and pupils. This will allow for the development of teachers' knowledge about children and young people's capacities to work with moving image (and other media texts), allowing for much clearer understandings of how to support and assess pupils' own work. This latter area will need some rigorous research into pupils' learning to underpin practice. As the examples above so amply demonstrate, some forms of practice are already rapidly evolving and are full of excitement and achievement for pupils and teachers alike.

Overall these changes are likely to occur either slowly or rapidly, depending on the curricular and assessment framework that will be their constraining or enhancing context; but occur they will. As a result, terms like 'creative' and 'imaginative' will be in the foreground of English teaching and the moving image will be central to their exploration and their development in pupils and teachers alike.

References

Abbs, P. (1982) *English within the Arts: A Radical Alternative for English and the Arts in the Curriculum*, London, Hodder and Stoughton.

Andrews, R. (2003) (ed.) *The Impact of ICT on Literacy Education*, London, Routledge Falmer.

Applebee, A. (1974) *Tradition and Reform in the Teaching of English: A History*, Urbana, IL, NCTE.

Barker, M. and Brooks, K. (1998) *Knowing Audiences: Judge Dredd, Its Friends, Fans and Foes*, Luton, University of Luton Press.

Bazalgette, C. (1989) *Primary Media Education: A Curriculum Statement*, London, British Film Institute.

Bazalgette, C., Earle, W., Grahame, J., Reid, M. and West, A. (eds) (2000) *Moving Images in the Classroom*, London, British Film Institute.

Beavis, C. (2001) 'Digital cultures: digital literacies', in Durrant, C. and Beavis, C. *P(ICT)ures of English: Teachers, Learners and Pedagogy*, AATE/Wakefield Press, Kent Town, South Australia.

Benn, C. and Chitty, C. (1996) *Thirty Years On: Is Comprehensive Education Alive and Well or Struggling to Survive?*, London, David Fulton.

Benton, P. (1996) 'Children's reading and viewing in the nineties', in Davies, C. *What is English Teaching?*, Buckingham, Open University Press.

BFI (1988) *Secondary Media Education: A Curriculum Statement*, London, British Film Institute.

BFI (1989) *Primary Media Education: A Curriculum Subject*, London, British Film Institute.

BFI (1999) *Making Movies Matter: Report of the Film Education Working Group*, London, British Film Institute.

BFI (2000) *Moving Images in the Classroom: A Secondary Teacher's Guide to Using Film and Television*, London, British Film Institute.

Bowker, J. (1989) *Secondary Media Education: A Curriculum Statement*, London British Film Institute.

Britton, J. (1970) *Language and Learning*, London, Penguin.

Britton, J., Shafer, R. and Watson, K. (1990) *Teaching and Learning English Worldwide*, Clevedon, Multilingual Matters.

Bruner, J. (1990) *Acts of Meaning*, Cambridge, MA, Harvard University Press.

Buckingham, D. (ed.) (1993a) *Reading Audiences: Young People and the Media*, Manchester, Manchester University Press.

Buckingham, D. (1993b) *Children Talking Television: The Making of Television Literacy*, London, Falmer.

Buckingham, D. (1996) *Moving Images: Understanding Children's Emotional Responses to Television*, Manchester, Manchester University Press.

Buckingham, D. (2000) *The Making of Citizens: Young People, News and Politics*, London, Routledge.

Buckingham, D. (2002) *After the Death of Childhood: Growing Up in the Age of Electronic Media*, Buckingham, Open University Press.

Buckingham, D., Grahame, J. and Sefton-Green, J. (1995) *Making Media: Practical Production in Media Education*, London, The English and Media Centre.

Buckingham, D., Harvey, G. and Sefton-Green, J. (19991) 'The difference is digital: digital technology and student media production', *Convergence*, Vol. 5, No. 4, Winter.

Burn, A. (2000) 'Creativity with moving images', in Bazalgette, C., Earle, W., Grahame, J., Reid, M. and West, A. (eds) *Moving Images in the Classroom*, London, British Film Institute.

Burn, A. (2003) 'ICT and moving image literacies', in Andrews, R. (ed.) *The Impact of ICT on Literacy Education*, London, Routledge Falmer.

Burn, A., Brindley, S., Durran, J., Kelsall, K., Sweetlove, J. and Tuohey, C. (2001) 'The rush of images: a research report into digital editing and the moving image', *English in Education*, Vol. 35, No. 2, Sheffield, National Association for the Teaching of English.

Burn, A. and Parker, D. (2001) 'Making your mark: digital inscription, animation, and a new visual semiotic', *Education, Communication and Information*, Vol. 1, 155–79.

Burn, A. and Reed, K. (1999) 'Digi-teens: media literacies and digital technologies in the secondary classroom', *English in Education*, Vol. 33, No. 3, Autumn, Sheffield, National Association for the Teaching of English.

Burn, A. and Schott, G. (2003) 'Heavy hero or digital dummy: multi-modal player–avatar relations in Final Fantasy 7'. Submitted for publication.

Burton, G. (2000) *Talking Television: An Introduction to the Study of Television*, London, Arnold.

Cope, B. and Kalantzis, M. (eds) (1993) *The Powers of Literacy: A Genre Approach to Teaching Writing*, London, Falmer.

Cope, B. and Kalantzis, M. (2000) *Multiliteracies: Literacy Learning and the Design of Social Futures*, London, Routledge.

DCMS (1998) *A Bigger Picture*, London, BFI/DCMS.

DES (1975) *A Language for Life* (The Bullock Report), London, HMSO.

DES (1989) *English for Ages 5–16* (The Cox Report), London, HMSO.

DES (1995) *English for Ages 5–16* (First major revision to the National Curriculum for English), London, HMSO.

DfES (2000) *English for Ages 5–16*, London, HMSO.

DfES (2002) *ImpaCT 2: The Impact of Information and Communication Technologies on Pupil Learning and Attainment*, London, HMSO.

Dick, B. (2002) *Anatomy of Film*, Boston, Beford/St Martin's.

Doughty, P., Pearce, J. and Thornton, G. (1971) *Language in Use* (Schools Council Programme in Linguistics and English teaching), London, Heinemann.

During, S. (1993) *The Cultural Studies Reader*, London, Routledge.

Durrant, C. and Beavis, C. (eds) (2001) *P(ICT)ures of English: Teachers, Learners and Pedagogy*, AATE/Wakefield Press, Kent Town, South Australia.

Eagleton, T. (1983) *An Introduction to Literary Theory*, Oxford, Basil Blackwell.

Ellis, V. and Robinson, M. (2000) 'Writing in English and responding to writing', in Sefton-Green, J. and Sinker, R. (eds) *Evaluating Creativity: Making and Learning by Young People*, London, Routledge.

Gee, J. (2000) 'New people in new worlds: networks, the new capitalism and schools', in Cope, B. and Kalantzis, M., *Multiliteracies: Literacy Learning and the Design of Social Futures*, London, Routledge.

Giddings, R., Selby, K. and Wensley, C. (1990) *Screening the Novel: The Theory and Practice of Literary Dramatization*, London, Macmillan.

Goodson, I. and Medway, P. (1990) *Bringing English to Order*, London, Falmer.

Goodson, I. (ed.) (1993) *School Subjects and Curriculum Change*, London, Falmer.

Goodwyn, A. (1992a) *English Teaching and Media Education*, Buckingham, Open University Press.

Goodwyn, A. (1992b) 'Theoretical models of English teaching', *English in Education*, Vol. 26, No. 3, Sheffield, The National Association for The Teaching of English.

Goodwyn, A. (ed.) (1995) *English and Ability*, London, David Fulton.

Goodwyn, A. (1997a) *Developing English Teachers: The Role of Mentorship in a Reflective Profession*, Buckingham, Open University Press.

Goodwyn, A. (1997b) 'Mother tongue or mother media?', paper given at The International Association for the Improvement of Mother Tongue Education, International Conference, The University of Amsterdam, July.

Goodwyn, A. (1997c), 'English teachers' theories of teaching' paper given at The International Association for the Improvement of Mother Tongue Education, International Conference, The University of Amsterdam, July.

Goodwyn, A. (ed.) (1998) *Literary and Media Texts in Secondary English*, London, Cassells.

Goodwyn, A. (ed.) (2000) *English in the Digital Age*, London, Continuum.

Goodwyn, A. (ed.) (2002a) *Improving Literacy at KS2 and KS3*, London, Sage.

Goodwyn, A. (2002b) 'Breaking up is hard to do: English teachers and that LOVE of reading', *English Teaching, Practice and Critique*, Vol. 1, No. 1, 66–78.

Goodwyn, A. (2003) 'Literacy or English: the struggle for the professional identity of English teachers in England', in *English Teachers at Work: Narratives, Counter-narratives and Arguments*, Kent Town, South Australia, AATE/Interface and Wakefield Press.

Goodwyn, A. and Findlay, K. (2001) 'Media Studies and the establishment', *The International Journal of Media Education*, Vol. 1, No. 1, 23–40.

Goodwyn, A. and Zancanella, D. (2003) 'How pre-service teachers in England and the United States view media literacy', paper given at the American Educational Research Association Conference, Chicago, IL.

Goodwyn, A., Adams, A. and Clarke, S. (1997) 'The great god of the future: English teachers and information technology', *English in Education*, Vol. 30, No. 2, Sheffield, The National Association for the Teaching of English.

Green, B. (ed.) (1993) *The Insistence of the Letter: Literacy Studies and Curriculum Theorizing*, London, Falmer.

Griffith, P. (1992) *English at the Core: Dialogue and Power in English Teaching*, Buckingham, Open University Press.

Haas-Dyson, A. (1997) *Writing Superheroes: Contemporary Childhood, Popular Culture and Classroom Literacy*, New York, Teachers College Press, Columbia University.

Halloran, J. and Jones, M. (1986) *Learning about the Media: Communication and Society* (UNESCO Papers), Paris, UNESCO.

Hart, A. and Benson, T. (1992) *Models of Media Education: A Study of Secondary English Teachers Teaching Media, Part 1, Overview, Occasional Papers, 11*, Southampton, Centre for Language in Education, University of Southampton.

Hart, A. and Benson, T. (1993) *Models of Media Education: A Study of Secondary English Teachers Teaching Media, Part 2, Profiles and Lessons, Occasional Papers, 12*, Southampton, Centre for Language in Education, University of Southampton.

Hart, A. and Hicks, A. (2002) *Teaching Media in the English Curriculum*, London, Trentham Books.

Harvey, I., Skinner, M. and Parker, D. (2002) *Being Seen, Being Heard: Young People and Moving Image Production*, London, British Film Institute/National Youth Agency.

Higgins, C. (2002) 'Using film text to support reluctant writers', *English in Education*, Vol. 36, No. 1, Sheffield, National Association for the Teaching of English.

Hurrel, G., Sommer, P. and Sarev, J. (2001) 'Cyber-English and the New Classroom Aliens?', in Durrant, C. and Beavis, C., *P(ICT)ures of English: Teachers, Learners and Pedagogy*, AATE/Wakefield Press, Kent Town, South Australia.

Inglis, F. (1990) *Media Theory: An Introduction*, Oxford, Blackwell.

Jones, K. and Buckingham, D. (2002) 'New Labour's cultural turn: some tensions in contemporary educational and cultural policy', *Journal of Education Policy*, Vol. 16, No. 1, 1–14.

Kenway, J. and Bullen, E. (2001) *Consuming Children: Education, Entertainment, Advertising*, Buckingham, Open University Press.

Kerr, P. (1982) 'Classic serials: to be continued', *Screen*, Vol. 23, No. 1, May/June.

Kress, G. (1995) *Writing the Future: English and the Making of a Culture of Innovation*, Sheffield, The National Association for the Teaching of English.

Kress, G. (2002) 'English for an era of instability: aesthetics, ethics, creativity and design', *English in Australia*, Vol. 134, 15–24.

Kress, G. (2003) *Literacy in the New Media Age*, London, Routledge.

Kress, G. and Van Leeuwen, T. (1996) *Reading Images: A Grammar of Visual Design*, London, Routledge.

Kress, G. and Van Leeuwen, T. (2001) *Multi-modal Discourse: The Modes and Media of Contemporary Communication*, Oxford, Oxford University Press.

Lanham, R. (1993) *The Electronic Word: Democracy, Technology and the Arts*, Chicago, IL, University of Chicago Press.

Lankshear, C. (1997) *Changing Literacies*, Buckingham, Open University Press.

Leavis, F.R. and Thompson, D. (1933) *Culture and Environment*, London, Chatto and Windus.

Lee, C. and Smagorinsky, P. (2000) *Vygotskian Perspectives on Literacy: Constructing Meaning through Collaborative Inquiry*, Cambridge, Cambridge University Press.

Lemin, K. (2001) 'Practical production work within an integrated English and Media curriculum: acquisition of theory or creative exploration?', *English in Education*, Vol. 35, No. 1, Sheffield, National Association for The Teaching of English.

Levy, M. and Gunter, B. (1988) *Home Video and the Changing Nature of the Television Audience*, London, John Libbey.

Livingstone, S. (2002) *Young People and New Media: Childhood and the Changing Media Environment*, London, Sage.

Marland, M. (ed.) (1977) *Language across the Curriculum*, London, Heinemann Educational.

Masterman, L. (1980) *Teaching about Television*, London, Macmillan.

Mathieson, M. (1975) *The Preachers of Culture*, London, Allen and Unwin.

Morgan, W. (1997) *Critical Literacy in the English Classroom: The Art of the Possible*, London, Routledge.

Murdock, G. and Phelps, G. (1973) *Mass Media and the Secondary School*, London, Allen and Unwin.

Myers, M. (1996) *Changing Our Minds: Negotiating English and Literacy*, Urbana, IL, The National Council of Teachers of English.

NACCCE (National Advisory Committee on Creative and Cultural Education) (1999) *All Our Futures: Creativity, Culture and Education*, London, DfEE.

Negroponte, N. (1995) *Being Digital*, London, Hodder and Stoughton.

Ofsted (2001) *ICT in Schools: The Impact of Government Initiatives*, London, HMSO.

Pirie, B. (1997) *Reshaping High School English*, Urbana, IL, NCTE.

Phillips, W. (2002) *Film: An Introduction*, Boston, MA, Bedford/St Martin's.

Postman, N. (1985) *Amusing Ourselves to Death: Public Discourse in the Age of Show Business*, London, Methuen.

Raney, K. (1999) 'A matter of survival: on being visually literate', *The English and Media Magazine*, No. 39, London, The English and Media Centre.

Reynolds, P. (ed.) (1993) *Novel Images: Literature in Performance*, London, Routledge.

Rice, J. and Saunders, C. (1996) 'Consuming Middlemarch: the construction and consumption of nostalgia in Stamford', in Cartmel, D., Hunter, I.Q., Kaye, H. and Whelan, I., *Pulping Ficions: Consuming Cultures across the Literature/Media Divide*, London, Pluto, pp. 85–98.

Sanders, B. (1995) *A is for Ox: The Collapse of Literacy and the Rise of Violence in an Electronic Age*, New York, Vintage.

Sanger, J. with Willson, J., Davies, B. and Whittaker, R. (1997) *Young Children, Videos and Computer Games: Issues for Teachers and Parents*, London, Falmer.

Scholes, R. (1985) *Textual Power: Literary Theory and the Teaching of English*, London, Yale University Press.

Schön, D. (1983) *The Reflective Practitioner: How Professionals Think in Action*, New York, Basic Books.

Schools Curriculum and Assessment Authority (1995) *GCSE Regulations and Criteria*, London, SCAA.

Sefton-Green, J. (2003a) 'Children's TV goes online', in Buckingham, D. (ed.) *Small Screens: Television for Children*, Leicester, Leicester University Press.

Sefton-Green, J. (2003b) 'Informal learning: substance or style?', *Teaching Education*, Vol. 13, No. 1.

Sefton-Green, J. and Sinker, R. (eds) (2000) *Evaluating Creativity: Making and Learning by Young People*, London, Routledge.

Shared Spaces Project, available online at http: //www.wac.co.uk/ sharedspaces/research.php (accessed 5 April 2003).

Shulman, L. (1986) 'Those who understand: knowledge growth in education', *Educational Researcher*, Vol. 15, 4–14.

Sinker, R. (2000) 'Making multimedia: evaluating young people's creative multimedia production', in Sefton-Green, J. and Sinker, R. (eds) *Evaluating Creativity: Making and Learning by Young People*, London, Routledge.

Stoneman, P. (1996) *Bronte Transformations: The Cultural Dissemination of Jane Eyre and Wuthering Heights*, Hemel Hempstead, Prentice Hall/ Harvester Wheatsheaf.

Thompson, E. (1996) *Sense and Sensibility: The Diaries*, London, Bloomsbury.

Thompson, J. (1996) '"Vanishing" worlds: film adaptation and the mystery of the original', in Cartmel, D., Hunter, I.Q., Kaye, H. and Whelan, I. *Pulping Fictions: Consuming Cultures Across the Literature/Media Divide*, London, Pluto, pp. 11–28.

Tuman, M. (1992) *Word Perfect: Literacy in the Computer Age*, London, Falmer.

Tweddle. S., Adams, A., Clarke, S., Scrimshaw, P. and Walton, S. (1997) *English for Tomorrow*, Buckingham, Open University Press.

Willett, R. (2003) 'New models for new media: young people learning digital culture', *Medienpädagogik*, Vol. 4.

Willis, P (1990) *Common Culture*, Buckingham, Open University Press.

Winn, M. (1977) *The Plug-In-Drug*, New York, Viking.

Zancanella, D., Hall, L. and Pence, P. (2000) 'Treating computer games as literature', in Goodwyn, A. (ed.), *English in the Digital Age*, London, Continuum, pp. 87–102.

Index